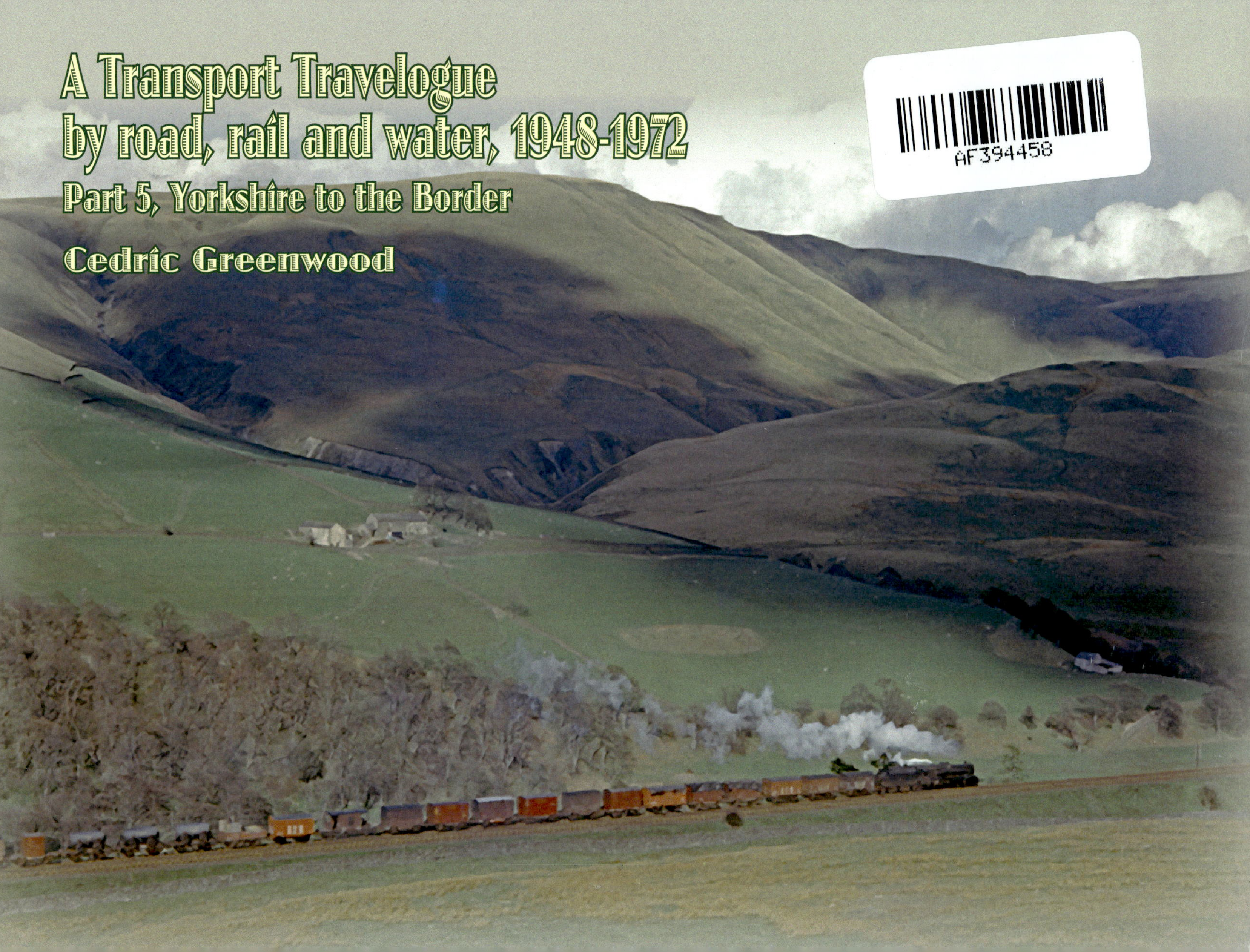
A Transport Travelogue
by road, rail and water, 1948-1972
Part 5, Yorkshire to the Border
Cedric Greenwood

© Cedric Greenwood 2018

All rights reserved. No part of this publication may be reproduced, stored in a retrieval system or transmitted, in any form or by any means, electronic, mechanical, photocopying, recording or otherwise, without prior permission in writing from Silver Link Publishing Ltd.

First published in 2018

British Library Cataloguing in Publication Data

A catalogue record for this book is available from the British Library.

ISBN 978 1 85794 501 0
Silver Link Publishing Ltd
The Trundle
Ringstead Road
Great Addington
Kettering
Northants NN14 4BW

Tel/Fax: 01536 330588
email: sales@nostalgiacollection.com
Website: www.nostalgiacollection.com

Printed and bound in the Czech Republic

Some of the pictures in this book appeared previously in the same author's *Echoes of Steam and Vintage Voltage* (Silver Link Publishing, 2015).

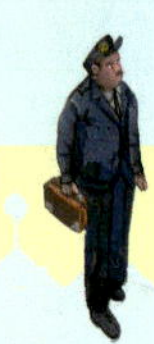

Acknowledgements

My thanks for making this series of books possible go to those who printed my black and white photographs: Ian Breckin of Silvertone, Leeds; Steve Howe of the Black & White Picture Place, Chester; and the late Ken Tyhurst of Canterbury.

Thanks also to those who processed my colour slides and prints: Fujifilm laboratories, Warwick; and CC Imaging Photo Lab, Leeds.

In writing the introductory text and captions I am indebted to the following people for information and assistance: Carol Donelly, Carlisle city guide; Ted Gadsby of Walsall, Omnibus Society librarian; Stuart McKenzie, British Waterways harbour master on the River Ouse; Nigel Mussett and Peter Shaw of the Fiends of the Settle & Carlisle Railway; Pat Rudrum of Holt, Norfolk, my Internet intermediary; Robert Sawyers, relief harbour master on the River Hull; and Tom Turner of Wallasey for help in identifying and dating motor vehicles.

I am also indebted for information to the staff of Associated British Ports at Hull; Haig Colliery Mining Museum, Whitehaven; Hull Maritime Museum; Norfolk County Libraries, for computer services at Holt; and Teesside Archives.

Title page: **LONSDALE** This sheep's-eye view shows a 'Black Five' leading a southbound freight through the Lune gap at Carlin Gill, the 'witch's ravine' in the background between the green pastures of Westmorland and the brown moors of Yorkshire, on 1 May 1963. Above the railway is High Carlingill Farm on the route of the Roman road from Lancaster to Carlisle, and at the top of the picture is Uldale Head (1,533 feet). The M6 motorway now runs along the slopes in the foreground on two levels.

Right: **NORTON WOODSEATS** Inside the upper saloon of a Sheffield standard tramcar of the 1930s approaching Woodseats along Abbey Lane on 17 July 1958. The passenger reposed on the front seat is Margaret Nicholls from Bishopsbourne, Kent, who, on a 16-day cycle tour of England and Wales, had dropped into Sheffield from the High Peak district of Derbyshire and 'changed horses' to get a grandstand view of the city from the comfort and security of a tramcar with its upholstered, leather seats and glassy upper saloon, just as Gladstone recommended seeing London from the top of a bus. The belt line along Abbey Lane formed a loop around the south end of the system linking Woodseats with Beauchief (pronounced 'Beech'f'). It was on a turfed, roadside reservation most of the way from Beauchief but the line closed seven months later. Trams operated a north-south cross-city route in both directions between Firth Park, Woodseats, Beauchief and Vulcan Road, only reversing at the north end.

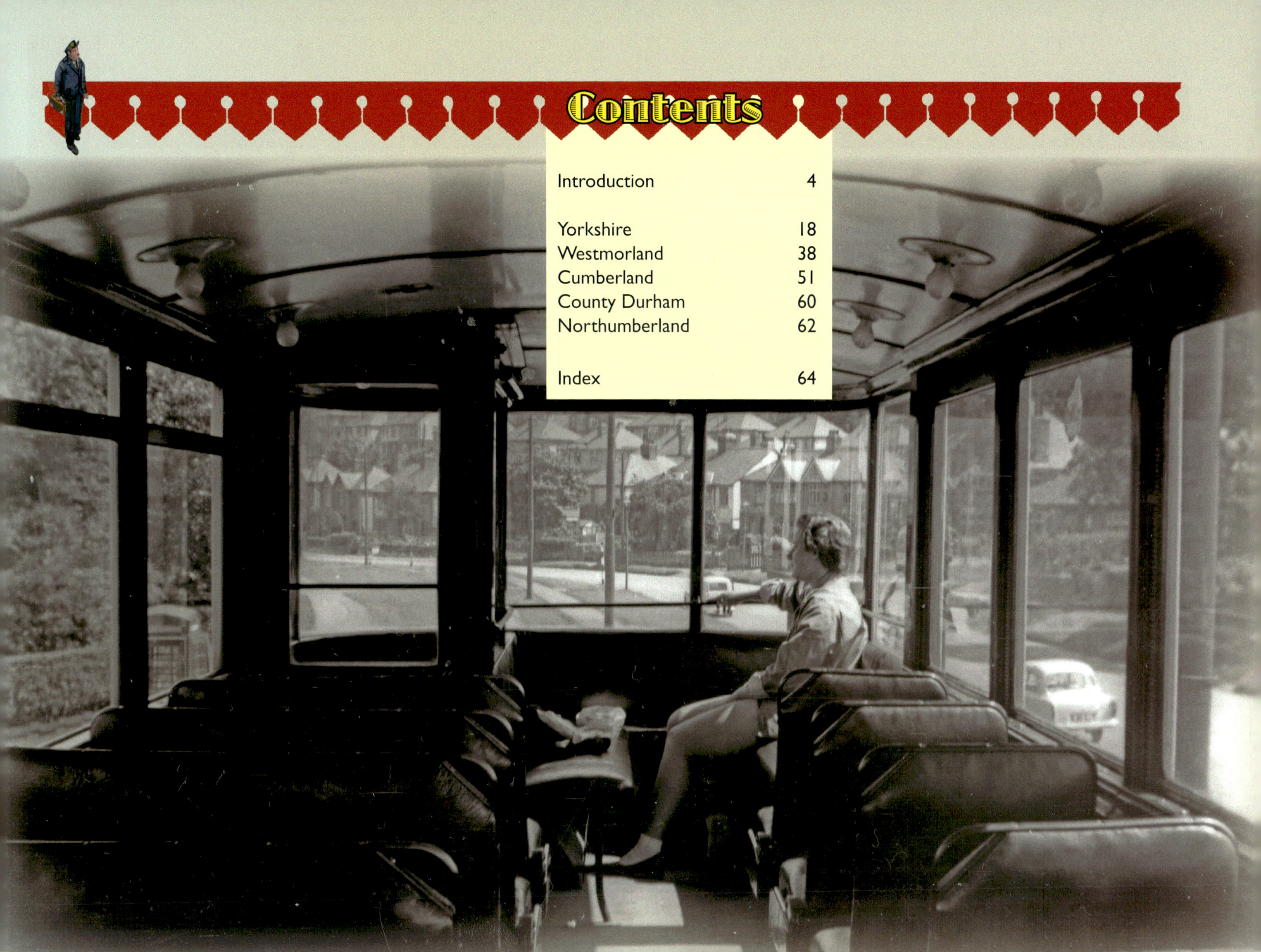

Contents

Introduction   4

Yorkshire   18
Westmorland   38
Cumberland   51
County Durham   60
Northumberland   62

Index   64

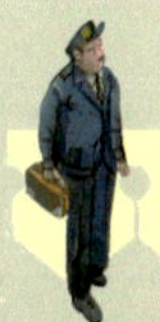

Introduction

We enter the north country at the port of Kingston-on-Hull, named after King Edward I's charter of 1299 but generally known by the name of its river – **Hull**. At the time of our review this was the third most important port in Britain, its 7 miles of docks along the north bank of the Humber exporting volumes of coal and textiles and importing mainly wool, wheat, timber, linseed and soya beans. It was also Britain's main base for deep-sea fishing. Barges from the Old Harbour on the River Hull and from the city docks on the Humber navigated the vast ramification of canalised rivers radiating far inland from the Humber across the flat vales of Trent and York to Lincoln, Nottingham, Sheffield, Leeds, York and Beverley, carrying mainly coal, grain, oil seed and timber.

Barge traffic declined in the 1970s as more cargoes went by road, and Hull has now declined to the 14th port of Britain in terms of cargo tonnage. It no longer has a fishing fleet, but fish is still landed here by foreign vessels. As at London and Liverpool the old city-centre docks have closed and trade has shifted to the larger docks up and down the Humber that have been modernised to handle bulk cargoes, containers and North Sea ferries. Motor barges still ply from these docks up the rivers and broad canals to Besthorpe (near Newark), Rotherham, Woodlesford (near Leeds) and Drax with cargoes of aggregates, fertilisers, fly-ash, gypsum, oil products, steel and timber.

Unless you're a mariner, Hull is not a place you would go to unless you have to because it is remotely situated on the end of a road to nowhere else, surrounded by miles of wide open spaces of corn prairies and grassy wolds on both sides of the Humber. It is situated in the East Riding of Yorkshire, the only one of the three former 'ridings' (from the Anglo-Saxon for 'thirdings') to retain its identity in modern times, which includes the Yorkshire Wolds and the plain of Holderness.

Yorkshire is by far the largest county in Britain and at the time of our survey it was divided into three ridings. The largest was the West Riding extending from Goole and Sheffield in the south-east up through all the woollen-mill towns, Nidderdale, Wharfedale and over the Pennine watershed to Ribblesdale, Whernside and Sedbergh in the north-west. The North Riding stretched from Scarborough in the east to the Pennine watershed between the heads of Wensleydale and Teesdale. The three ridings met at York. After the reshuffles of local government in 1974 and 1996, and after 22 years as part of a new county of Humberside, the East Riding of Yorkshire has been restored to its old self. We now have a South Yorkshire and a West Yorkshire (sic), which are collections of autonomous industrial boroughs from Sheffield to Bradford, while North Yorkshire (sic) is an expansion of the old North Riding, taking in York and all the Yorkshire dales, except for Dentdale and Garsdale, which have been ceded to the new county of Cumbria. I mention the old ridings out of interest, but I am treating Yorkshire as a whole, like Lincolnshire (which had three parts) and Sussex (two).

In the field of transport Yorkshire was distinguished by having more **trolleybus systems** than any other area of Britain of like size: ten municipal and one company. Eight of them were in the West Riding, and seven of these survived into our review period of 1948-72. Bradford and Leeds pioneered trolleybuses in Britain, both inaugurating services on 20 June 1911, and Bradford's was also the last trolleybus system in Britain to close, in 1972. Rotherham opened Britain's third trolleybus system in 1912. Both Rotherham Corporation and its northern neighbour, Mexborough & Swinton Traction Company, had fleets of only single-deck trolleybuses because of low railway bridges on their joint service, although in 1956 Rotherham converted some of its vehicles to double-deckers for local routes. Teesside opened the last new trolleybus route extension in Britain in 1968 and was the last but one system to close, in 1971. Closing dates of the other Yorkshire trolleybus systems in our period were Mexborough & Swinton (1961), Doncaster (1963), Hull (1964), Rotherham (1965) and Huddersfield (1968).

Sheffield was the last city in England to close its tramway system. The last route to close, on 8 October 1960, typified the extremes of Sheffield, linking Vulcan Road down among the steel works in the industrial Don valley with Millhouses and Beauchief in the salubrious, sylvan, south-western suburbs on the edge of the Peak District moors. Lines west and north climbed into those moors with steep, narrow winding streets, which were photogenic tramscapes, but those lines had closed before I visited Sheffield.

One could usually identify a town in a black and white photograph by the style of its tramcars. Many tramway undertakings built most of their tramcars in their own workshops on running gear with electric equipment supplied by specialist firms. Sheffield Corporation built most its pre-war standard trams in Queen's Road workshops: 61-seat four-wheelers on Peckham trucks with clean body lines and bowed ends slightly flattened. Sheffield was bold in painting its trams in a mainly ivory colour scheme, trimmed dark blue, in a smoky, industrial environment, but it always kept them clean and shiny.

Thus Sheffield had a tramway of some character. In the 1950s eight lines radiated from the city centre, linked up by five orbital lines and leading to 13 outer terminals. The tramcars ran almost right around the clock; the first car left the city centre just after 3.00am and the last returned to the city shortly after 2.00am. The sight, sound and motion of the electric cars climbing gas-lit – and unlit – empty streets in the late and early hours was a ghostly experience.

This busy, efficient system was popular with the citizens, who were vociferous in their opposition to its closure. The tramlines were made in Sheffield and the electric power was generated locally, not imported like bus diesel fuel. The lines were closed one by one from 1952 to 1960 in a city council programme to replace electric trams with diesel buses. However, the last tram to run was not Sheffield's last. In 1994 the city joined the tramway renaissance in Britain with the opening of a 15-mile nucleus of a new tramway system with modern, low-floor, articulated single-deckers on street tracks and reservations. Three lines radiate from the city centre to five suburban terminals, including Middlewood and Malin Bridge on the old system, but not yet to any of the locations pictured herein.

I kept diaries of interesting journeys in the 1950s and '60s and here is my description of a journey by Sheffield tram from High Street to Vulcan Road on 19 May 1959:

'The tram descended the hill on which the city centre stands, crossed the bridge over the river Don, here banked by the sheer walls of factories

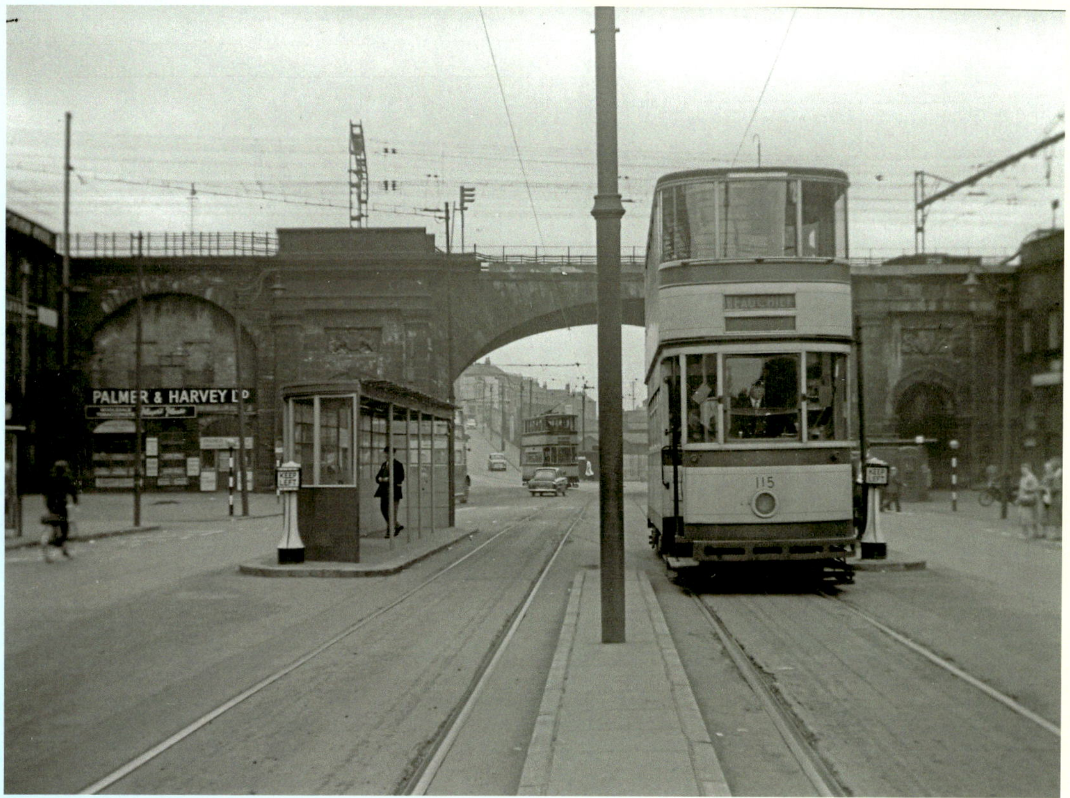

SHEFFIELD Trams to Vulcan Road, Brightside and Sheffield Lane Top divided after passing under the Wicker Arches, the viaduct carrying the electrified lines of the ex-Great Central Railway. This picture shows standard car 115, one of 68 cars built in 1930-33, southbound from Vulcan Road to Beauchief. In the background a northbound standard car forks left for the climb to Sheffield Lane Top. The route from Vulcan Road, Tinsley, to Millhouses and Beauchief was the last tram route in Sheffield and closed on 8 October 1960.

The railway, also with overhead electric wires, was on the route from Manchester London Road to Sheffield Victoria via Penistone, and was the only British railway electrified at 1,500 volts AC. Electrification was completed to Sheffield in 1955 and extended for freight to Tinsley in 1965, but the route closed to passengers in 1970 and to freight in 1981. All trains between Sheffield and Manchester are now routed by the non-electric ex-Midland line via Dore and Chinley.

and warehouses, and we headed north-east through Attercliffe and Carrbrook to Tinsley. This was the home of Sheffield steel, a land of huge, black, grim buildings with tall chimney stacks spitting flames and belching, variously, black, blue, red and yellow plumes of smoke. They stand among gigantic slag heaps, railway marshalling yards, scummy canals and the torrential rivers that drove the first water-powered hammer mills of the district.

Sections of the route are lined with small, soot-black workers' houses and shabby little shops with old fashioned, worn, enamelled steel advertising plaques. In one place a small crowd gathered around the entrance of an alley in which two men were fighting. In the background are steep hillsides, furrowed with more streets of slum houses.

The character of the scene is forbidding and barbaric and I looked with awe at the sight of heavy industry such as I had never seen before. Almost everywhere I looked there was a fascinating view from the top deck of the tramcar. At Tinsley, 3½ miles from the city centre, where the road leaves the built-up area and traverses a desolate, desecrated landscape to Rotherham, the tramcar turned left into Vulcan Road to terminate alongside Hadfield's steel works, where they made and prefabricated tramway track layouts for street junctions and depot trackfans.'

This route to Tinsley once linked up through Templeborough with the Rotherham tramways, and a joint tram service operated between Sheffield and Rotherham till 1948. For this service Rotherham Corporation used single-ended double-deckers with bodies like trolleybuses. Thus each car had only one entrance, one staircase and fixed seats, like any bus, so passengers rode backwards in one direction! There is a scheme to extend the new Sheffield tramways from Meadowhall to Rotherham via the railway.

That visit to Sheffield was on a 1,812-mile **hitch-hiking** and youth-hostelling tour of midland and northern England and Scotland in 16 days with my girlfriend and wife-to-be, Ruth Amos, from Kent, who had never ridden in the cabs of lorries or seen trams or heavy industry before; I think, to her at that age (she was 19), it was either a culture shock or a novel adventure, or both.

Continuing my diary entry for that day we see how easy hitch-hiking was then, and how drivers went out of their way to help others:

'We spent six hours in Sheffield, riding the trams and shopping. We travelled in six trams for 17 miles on four of the five remaining routes, finally alighting at Parkside Road on the line to Wadsley Bridge.

We walked up the cold, grey streets to join the A616 to Holmfirth and passed a big blue lorry from Liverpool we had seen in Sheffield earlier that day, standing outside a café. As we were fairly cold we went into the café for a mug of steaming hot tea. The Liverpool lorry driver, seeing us with our rucksacks and assuming we were travelling rough, offered us a lift. He said he could take us "a little way up the road to the crossroads". His soft, sing-song Merseyside accent was lovely to hear among the dour, gruff West Yorkshire accents. He drove us in his lorry for 11 miles north-west, bowling fearlessly on the narrow, rolling road through Oughtibridge and Deepcar and out on to the stern, wild, Pennine Moors and chilly-looking expanses of water in the Sheffield and Barnsley reservoirs to Langsett crossroads, 915 feet high on Thurlstone Moors, where he dropped us and turned west for Liverpool.'

There was another incident on the southbound leg of the journey through Yorkshire, near Ripon, where a psychic Liverpool lorry driver stopped for us on his own initiative after he saw us getting out of a car at a remote crossroads, guessing we would want

another lift, and he took us 6 miles further on our way.

On 20 May 1959, following a visit to Thornbury trolleybus depot to see a restored Bradford tramcar:

'...we boarded a dark blue double-deck bus of Samuel Ledgard, an independent operator, and rode nine miles for only 10d down the gradual eastern slopes of the Pennines to Leeds. The route was most devious and interesting. The bus took the most unlikely road at nearly every junction and we could not guess which way it would turn next. Thus we had an intimate tour of the Bradford-Leeds suburbia and countryside. The bus charged boldly and energetically up and down narrow, winding roads and around reflex-angled corners through dark grey, rugged townships and hamlets, over bare hills about 400 feet high, past gleaming, grey pools, over rushing streams, and entered Leeds by a back-street route past ironworks, over railway bridges and along streets of warehouses, terminating suddenly and unexpectedly in an unlikely place in a side street near City Square.'

Leeds was the centre of the cloth industry and was wholly soot-stained, drab and grim but relieved by the kaleidoscope of colours of the **buses**, for this city was also the most common point of convergence of bus routes in all Yorkshire and the paint schemes in those days were tasteful blends of rich, warm colours. Here we could see the buses of three corporations (Leeds, Bradford and Sheffield), one Tilling group company (West Yorkshire Road Car), two British Electric Traction group companies (East Yorkshire Motor Services and Yorkshire Woollen District Traction) and seven independent companies (South Yorkshire Motors, T. Burrows & Sons, Yorkshire Traction, West Riding Automobile, Kippax Motors, Hebble Motor Services and Samuel Ledgard). Leeds Corporation trams and buses were previously blue and white, but from 1950 the trams were repainted crimson and the buses dusky green. The West Riding Automobile Company had light red buses on its former tram routes and dark green buses on original bus routes. Thirteen of these bus firms terminated in Leeds Central Bus Station, but the eight remaining independents terminated in six different side streets, at one railway station and on one bombed site in the central area.

The variety of bus colours in Leeds was enhanced by the variety of **tramcars** in the post-war period when other cities were disposing of their cars. Leeds had a cosmopolitan fleet of native cars of its own designs supplemented by second-hand cars from Hull, London, Manchester and Southampton, though not quite all at the same time. These second-hand cars came in different shapes and colours from their native cities and many of them retained their native paint schemes in service in Leeds until they were repainted in the uniform colours of the Corporation.

In the heyday of the system, before 1953, Boar Lane was probably the busiest tram street in Britain with continuous lines of slow moving trams in both directions between City Square tramways centre and the Corn Exchange in Duncan Street, slowed by the intersection of Briggate with its long island loading platforms. It is said that there were no official stopping places in Boar Lane because the trams were moving so slowly that passengers could board and alight anywhere. At the time of the Coronation in 1953 Leeds introduced two royal-purple single-deck bogie cars with modern technology as prototypes

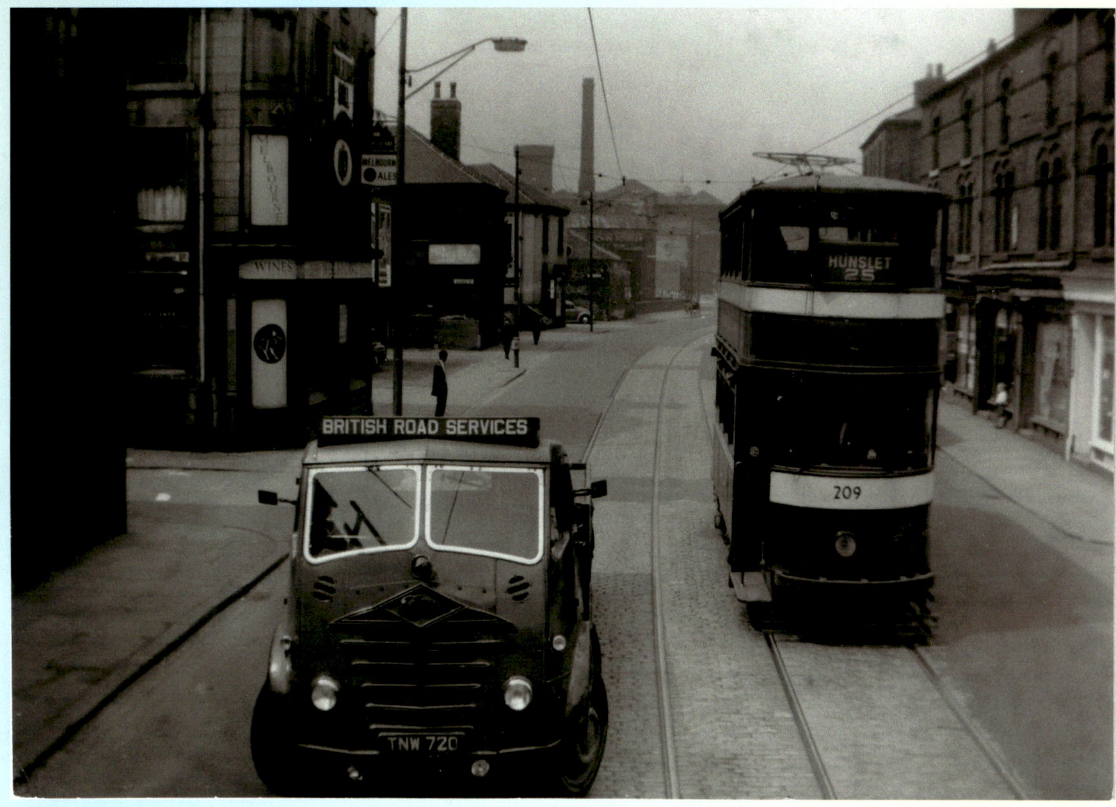

LEEDS Entering the city from the south-east on the top deck of a tramcar in Hunslet Road we meet the standard Leeds Corporation tramcar of the period bound for Hunslet and passing a 1954 Foden lorry waiting to reverse into a side street on 15 July 1958. The 'Horsfield' tramcars were designed by the tramways' General Manager, Mr R. L. Horsfield; the first four were built in the Corporation workshops and another 100 by Brush of Loughborough, all on Peckham trucks, in 1930-31. They were 60-seat cars with two 50hp motors per car and air brakes. From 1938 Leeds used bow collectors instead of trolley poles for a more secure contact with the overhead wire, as trolley wheels and skids could dewire at junctions. The Hunslet line closed on 18 April 1959. This view was taken from an ex-London 'Feltham' class car inbound from Middleton.

for a tram subway scheme in the city centre, but public transport here, as at Sheffield, was a matter of party politics and only four months later a new Labour city council began scrapping the tramways and the last cars ran to Temple Newsam and Cross Gates on 1 November 1959. The closure of this system seemed short-sighted in view of the miles of reserved tracks all around the city and the potential to reduce traffic congestion, air pollution and the then threat of a post-oil future.

Leeds was on the former **Midland Railway** main line from London St Pancras to Carlisle Citadel, with through running over the North British Railway to Edinburgh and the Glasgow & South Western Railway to Glasgow. In our period it was the route of the 'Thames-Clyde Express' and the 'Starlight Specials', but the limitations of post-1996 franchising have robbed this route of its use for through passenger services between Leeds and Glasgow.

North-west of Leeds the **Settle-Carlisle line**, with its fine landscapes and restored stone stations, is a favourite route for excursion trains with preserved steam locomotives. This is the highest main line in England, forging a dramatic passage over the western flanks of the North Pennine Moors and through the dales of Yorkshire, Westmorland and Cumberland in a marathon of gargantuan earthworks, 17 viaducts and 14 tunnels to maintain ruling gradients of 1 in 100 on each side of the summit at 1,169 feet. Railwaymen called it the '**Long Drag**', and it was a long drag whichever way you went over it with a steam freight train: 15 miles at 1 in 100 north from Settle to Blea Moor and the same again south from Ormside to Ais Gill.

I first rode this line on a 'Starlight Special' from St Pancras to Glasgow St Enoch in August 1956. I wrote this description of the journey through Yorkshire and northern England:

'North of Sheffield we ran through railway marshalling yards in the hazy glow of floodlights, past the silhouettes of large mills with all their windows lit up and through rumbling steel works with flaring smokestacks and glares from the forges – yet I saw no people about, not even engine crews or shunters. It seemed as if the railway freight operations and the factories were working by themselves; it was all rather eerie.

Beyond Leeds the train headed north-west and began a 55-mile climb up Airedale and Ribblesdale to the roof of England. The moon shone on the sleeping farmhouses and winding moorland roads. Over the stone walls I could discern the dark shapes of sleeping cows and sheep. The ascent culminated in a tunnel under Blea Moor. We emerged into Dentdale and ran slowly through Dent station, the highest in England. All the stations up here are small and quaint, built of rock-faced Pennine stone and remotely situated far from any visible habitation. The station oil lamps were extinguished and each station looked like a setting for "The Ghost Train".

The train laboured on up hill and down dale with viaducts and tunnels through the bleak moorland to Ais Gill summit on the watershed boundary between Yorkshire and Westmorland. Dawn broke on the fast, thrilling run down the wide, verdant valley of the River Eden, with moors and mountains on each side, and we followed the river to Carlisle. The stone-walled Citadel station still looked the same as it did in the old pictures of it about 1900, when trains of seven railway companies converged on this great, strategic, border junction.'

I was a newspaper reporter at Kendal, Westmorland, from 1963 to 1968 and it was quite by luck that I found myself in a grandstand seat for the **final theatre of steam on British Railways in 1967-68.** It seemed fitting that the steam age on the railways should stage its finale in the area of grimy, heavy industry and rugged, majestic fell country between Crewe and Carlisle, the Pennines and the Irish Sea. Steam locomotives migrated up here as they were now banned on the LNWR main line south of Crewe owing to the low clearances of the overhead electric wires. The last steam workings, freight and passenger, were over the Settle-Carlisle railway and lines radiating from Preston to Burnley, Liverpool, Blackpool, Barrow, Windermere and Carlisle.

The Settle-Carlisle line ran through the eastern edge of my news area and I spent many days off on my motor scooter – which was ideal for those narrow, stone-walled lanes – photographing and tape-recording the trains and interviewing the signalmen in those lonely cabins from Selside to Mallerstang.

They told me of high winds and snowdrifts affecting the operation of trains. The winds across these exposed uplands sometimes stripped the tarpaulins off trains of sheeted lime wagons and they ended up on the farms. Drifting snow in cuttings could halt slow, heavy freight trains and accumulate up to the arches of the road bridges. Trains could be stuck in snow for days while gangs of men dug them out each day only to find next morning that more snow had filled it all in again overnight. These deep snowdrifts in cuttings had to be shovelled out by hand before a snowplough could reopen the line.

The station master at Ribblehead, Bill Sharpe, was also an official weather observer for the Met Office. In December 1954 he recorded 5 inches of rain in one day, and in December 1964 he recorded a wind speed of 96mph, which blew eight new motorcars off a train of flatcars on Ribblehead Viaduct. It was night and the scene was illuminated by the saloon lights as the car doors had been flung open. Strong headwinds sometimes brought freight trains to a standstill on this exposed, quarter-mile-long, 165-foot-high viaduct at the head of Ribblesdale. The trains then had to be split and pulled into the sidings at Blea Moor half at a time.

Bill had to measure snow with a ruler but that was not easy in January 1963 when Ribblehead station was buried up to the roof in the stuff, and he dug a tunnel through it from his house to the station office. The line was blocked for a week, mainly by a 60-foot snowdrift over the north portal of Blea Moor Tunnel, and a freight train was stranded on the gradient up Mallerstang. With no station duties, Bill helped on the snowploughs for 24 hours at a time. Two engines were coupled together, with a snowplough at each end, and charged into the drifts with the firemen shovelling hard and the drivers pulling the injectors well out, creating a lot of black smoke.

I went up to the 'Long Drag' winter and summer in 1965, '66 and '67. In winter the cold air made the steam show up in voluminous white clouds for the photographs. In summer it was a place of sublime peace for the pilgrim on foot. Winter or summer, a day up on the line, with the wide open spaces, the sheep, the curlews, the great viaducts striding across the ravines, the lonely, oil-lit, wooden signal cabins, the railway 'characters' and the steam locomotives piling their smoke into the low cloud, was always a great tonic. The landscape it runs through is unchanged and the stations have been beautifully restored as in Midland Railway days, but steam locomotives no longer pound this beat, the station goods yards and signal cabins have gone, together with the railway 'characters', and so, for me, the railway has lost its romance. Here was a case of the railway enhancing the landscape but now the motorcars and motorcycles that line these moorland roads at weekends despoil the landscape and the solitude their owners go to seek.

Back at Kendal, on the A6 trunk route from London to Carlisle, the heavy traffic in lorries was the main concern. The A6 ran right through the centre of almost every town and city on the route in those days before bypasses and motorways and the route was a gauntlet of narrow streets and bridges, hazards and 'black spots', like a training course for advanced drivers. Immediately north of Kendal was the tortuous and notorious south ascent of Shap Fells, the scene of many a runaway lorry with brake failures that ended with me reporting them in the Magistrates' Court at Kendal. Some cases ended up in the coroner's court.

I described the Shap road in this diary extract of 22 May 1959, when Ruth and I hitch-hiked from Skipton to Glasgow on our tour of Britain, little suspecting that we would move home to Kendal three years later:

'By the bridge over the River Kent at the south end of town we stopped a fish merchant's lorry going home to Fife and it took us exactly 100 miles north to Abington in Lanarkshire. The first stage of this journey was the long ascent up the south side of the bleak, stern Shap Fells (1,986 feet), linking the North Pennine Moors with the Cumbrian Mountains. As we climbed steadily higher and higher on the steep, arduous, heaving road, the vast, grey-green, sweeping fells appeared to rear up enigmatically higher and evermore breathtakingly one behind the other, divided by yawning, empty dales. On the last stretch of the road to the summit there was before us a long line of about 50 lorries crawling steadily with their heavy loads up the gradient. This is the great west road route from England to Scotland but it seemed to be used mostly by lorries as only one car passed us on our way over Shap Fells. The A6 reaches a summit 1,397 feet high where the bleak, grey wastes are scarred with quarries for red granite, grey limestone and blue slate.'
In winter the Shap road was often impassable with ice and snowdrifts. The problem was the same as on the 'Long Drag' railway: heavy, slow-moving freights getting snowed up in the strong winds. Most winters saw the Shap Road closed and the lorries parked along the streets of Kendal and Penrith for days and nights on end, waiting till the weather abated and the road could be ploughed and reopened. Conditions did not improve until the new M6 took an easier route following the West Coast Main Line via Tebay in 1970.

My local railway at Kendal was the branch line from Oxenholme to Windermere, which eventually transpired to be the last steam-worked branch line on BR right up to the end of commercial steam traction in August 1968. It is interesting to note that, although BR promised to dieselise all the passenger services on the branch from 1 March 1965, there were so many breakdowns of diesel locomotives and multiple units that the date was postponed to 2 June 1965, then to 18 April 1966, when a DMU from the closed Carlisle-Silloth branch entered local service between Windermere, Kendal and Carnforth and through trains to and from Preston, Manchester and Crewe were diesel hauled. On the fifth day of the new diesel service a 'Black Five' hauled the express from London along the branch after the diesel locomotive had broken down.

Hundreds more steam passenger trains ran on the branch after the official 'last steam train' on 16 April 1966. On 26 January 1967 I noted four steam engines simultaneously from the footbridge spanning Kendal freight yard: an Ivatt 'Mogul' shunting the yard, a 'Black Five' arriving with a freight from Windermere, another 'Black Five' with a parcels train from the south, and a steam passenger train climbing the main line on yonder fellside north of Oxenholme.

A railwayman told me there was not enough new diesel stock available and there was a big turnover in new diesel locomotives and multiple units breaking down or catching fire so frequently that steam – mainly 'Black Fives' and 'Britannias' – still dominated the railways north of Crewe. In the event, the last steam passenger train to Windermere ran on 29 July 1968 – three years and four months after the first 'last steam train'. The last steam freight to Windermere was on 2 August 1968, and on 3 August the same engine, No 44709, performed the final steam shunting rites in Kendal yard.

That Saturday evening the last steam passenger trains on BR's standard gauge ran from Preston to Liverpool Exchange, headed by a 'Black Five', and that was really the end of the steam age.

One week later BR ran a 'Farewell to Steam' excursion from Liverpool to Manchester, Settle and Carlisle and back, using three 'Black Fives' and a 'Britannia' for different stages, all stabled and prepared at Carnforth, the last steam shed, which then closed. BR placed a ban on all steam operations on its metals – except the Vale of Rheidol narrow-gauge railway it still owned at Aberystwyth. As we know, this ban was later relaxed for privately promoted steam excursions, which are still operated occasionally on designated routes.

One two-car DMU from the closed Carlisle-Silloth line was sufficient to work all the local passenger services between Carnforth, Kendal and Windermere, and passengers from the branch had to change at Carnforth for the though services they had previously enjoyed to Preston, Manchester, Crewe and London. The DMUs we rode between Carnforth and Windermere were the oldest kind, built at Derby

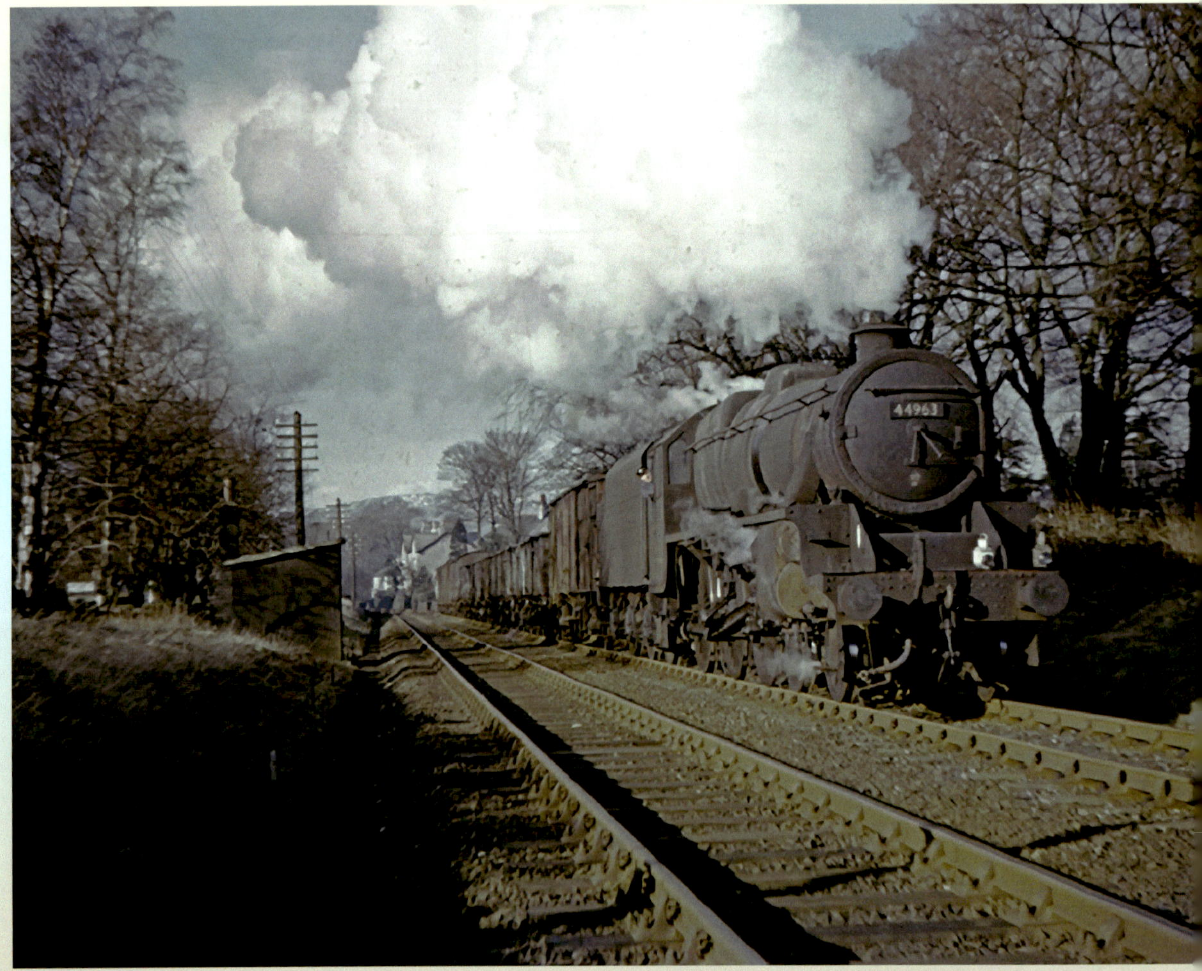

KENDAL 'Black Five' No 44963 (Horwich, 1946) climbs the 1 in 80 gradient out of Kendal towards Oxenholme with the early-afternoon freight to Carnforth on 14 February 1958.

in 1954-55 and rather like classic North American interurban electric cars in appearance: upright, polygonal ends, three large, deep cab windows at the front and a high-domed roof with a headlamp, although the resemblance to an American interurban was dispelled by the growling noise and the trail of oil smoke they left in the air. If you rode in the trailer car it was a smooth, quiet ride and swayed with a somewhat tramcar-like motion along the 60-foot-section track. The view from the passenger saloon through the motorman's cab was fascinating; we never had this view of the line before. On the run back from Carnforth to Kendal the fells gradually closed in around us and the countryside on the southern approaches to Kendal looked rich green and idyllic in the evening sunshine.

Steam's last duty in those final months of steam was on freight. There were only six classes of steam locomotive extant: the BR Standard 4MTs (mixed traffic), 5MTs, 7MTs ('Britannias') and 9Fs (freight), and two ex-LMSR classes, which, surviving from the mid-1930s, were a tribute to their designer, Sir William Stanier: the 5MT 'Black Five' 4-6-0s and the 8F 2-8-0s. The 'Black Five' was the 'maid of all work'. It proved to be economical, easy to maintain and capable of working any train from a loose-coupled goods to an express passenger over any route, and had a top speed of 90mph. A total of 841 of these locomotives were built by the LMSR and BR at Derby, Crewe and Horwich, by Vulcan at Newton-le-Willows, and Armstrong Whitworth at Newcastle from 1934 to 1951.

Stanier was Chief Mechanical Engineer of the LMSR from 1932 to 1944 and formerly the Great Western works manager at Swindon. He took with him the design features of the successful GWR 'Hall' and 'Castle' Class 4-6-0s, which could be seen in his 'Black Fives' and 8Fs with their tapered boilers and made them favourites among engine crews for their reliability and among enthusiasts for their ruggedly

handsome appearance. Both types succeeded many later BR Standard types to become the most numerous classes of steam locomotive in steam's final years. The 'Black Five' did the honours on BR's last regular passenger and freight duties and the final steam excursion, and No 44709 was the last steam locomotive on the Windermere branch.

BR's Standard 9F 2-10-0, built at Swindon and Crewe in 1954-60, was the last, the most powerful and the most successful large steam freight locomotive of all. It was ideal for iron ore drags from Birkenhead to Shotton, Tyne Dock to Consett and Newport to Ebbw Vale. It was even used on passenger trains, giving speeds up to 80-90mph on its 5-foot-diameter driving wheels. With the decision to end steam traction on BR by 1968, they were all scrapped prematurely, the first of them with more than two decades of work left in them; the last 9Fs were retired in 1967 after only seven years' service.

Those last three years of BR steam, when I photographed it and tape-recorded it in the north-western fell country, were the highlight of my transport experience. I was bent on recording the whole repertoire of sounds of the remaining steam passenger and freight operations on BR while there was still time. I captured all this repertoire, from the echoing voice of the station announcer right through to the engine crew coaling and watering the tender in the shed yard after a day's duty. I liked to hear the locomotive whistles echoing in the fells, their clanking side rods and squealing flanges in the freight yard and the sounds of shunting. This was all music to my ears. I communed with the locomotives, getting close up to capture their more intimate sounds. When they moved at walking speed the sound of squealing flanges that I coveted was broken down to a series of deep grunts and the earth trembled underfoot.

I recorded steam from the trackside, from the leading coach, from the locomotive footplate, from

the brake van on freight, from the signal cabin, under the coaling tower and even inside a tunnel. I recorded interviews with signalmen on the high and lonely reaches of the Settle-Carlisle line. I was on hand to record a classic wheelslip when a locomotive took 4 minutes to start moving out of Kendal freight yard in the early-morning dew. I sometimes rose at 4.00am in my quest for steam, and twice rode on the footplate on night freights over Shap to Carlisle and back with only two hours' sleep before going to the office next morning. I recorded these two trips on the footplate of 'Black Five' No 44817 from Oxenholme on 10 May 1967 and on 'Britannia' No 70012 *John of Gaunt* from Carnforth on 14 December 1967 – which I was told afterwards was the last steam freight over Shap. I also recorded one of the last runs of the last named steam passenger service on BR, the 'Belfast Boat Express', from Manchester Victoria to Heysham Harbour, both from the leading coach and on the locomotive, 'Black Five' No 45390, on 20 January 1968. These recordings, now on narrated compact disc programmes, bring the steam era back to life in a way that photographs can never do.

I was lucky to meet friendly railwaymen who willingly facilitated me in my quest to record these sounds for posterity in those last years of commercial steam traction. There was no more exciting way, especially from the aural aspect, of watching the trains go by than from a signal cabin, with its various bell codes and slamming levers, and I was accorded hospitality in every cabin I visited.

I also found I could hitch a ride on the footplate of a steam locomotive almost anywhere in the north west of England. There was no more exciting and satisfying way to travel than on a coal-fed iron horse with its barking blastpipe and pulsating motion, bells and buzzers foretelling the signals ahead and the fireman shovelling coal from the tender and swinging it into the hungry furnace. I was the third man on the footplate, clinging on to the cab side as the floors of the locomotive and tender moved different ways, and I was constantly regulating the volume control on my tape recorder for the high-decibel rumbling, grinding, squealing, clattering and wheezing.

My first footplate recording was on 'Black Five' No 45193 taking a freight up the 1 in 80 bank from Kendal to Oxenholme on 30 March 1967. The driver, Watson Sowerby of Carnforth, became a good friend and offered to take me with him anywhere and any time he was driving. Watson was originally at Kirkby Stephen East shed, which had closed, and his Westmorland accent distinguished him from the other Carnforth drivers. On 7 April 1967 I was travelling with him on the late-afternoon freight from Kendal to Burneside and back on Stanier 8F No 48438. After shunting the paper mill siding we were on our way back to Kendal with six trucks and the brake van when he gave me brief instructions on the operation of the vacuum and steam brakes, the regulator and the forward and reverse gear. I thought he was telling me out of interest, but he left me to stop the train on the up line opposite Kendal freight yard, where he got down from the footplate with his flask of tea and disappeared into the shunter's hut.

I then had to run the engine around the train, using two crossovers, take the train over on to the down line, propel it into the yard, shunt it in sections into the sidings, make up a new train and back it down gently on to the vans being loaded in the goods warehouse for Watson to take the train away to Carnforth. This I did on my own under the supervision of the fireman and the directions of the shunter, who did most of the work, signalling with his arms and uncoupling and coupling up the wagons. I was driving the locomotive for about 15 or 20 minutes. I recalled an engine driver saying: 'Anyone can drive an engine but it's stopping it in the right place that counts.'

The engine crews told me a lot of other things: about how BR recruited into management ex-army officers and matriculated management students, with no railway experience or inherent interest. It invested in a succession of different and untried new diesel locomotives, which proved to be unreliable. It seemed to be deliberately pricing itself out of the freight business and if it wanted to close a line it would run passenger trains at inconvenient times, but not when they were most needed, and repaint all the stations to add to the deficit.

In those last few months of steam I went down to Kendal freight yard almost every day to 'commune with the engines'. I felt completely satisfied and at one with the world as I wandered about the yard, sniffing the steam and listening to the squealing flanges of the locomotives, the 'dank-donk' of their coupling roads and the 'clink-clank' of the shunted wagons. I imbibed the sights, sounds and smells to refresh my soul and implant the memory for the future, which looked bleak.

Life after steam was an anti-climax. Some years later steam returned with tourist trains on preserved railways with a 25mph speed limit and steam excursions on BR metals, but I never tape-recorded any of these as they lacked the authenticity and urgency of commercial railway operation. However, I could still record the authentic operations of commercial steam railways in industry, which lasted a few years longer.

From Kendal my news area extended east to Garsdale, south to Grange-over-Sands, north to Ullswater and west to Ravenglass. The Cumbrian Mountains were a source of numerous minerals, notably granite, coal, iron ore, slate, lead and copper, which gave rise to local industries within and around the Lake District, served by their own railways, as illustrated herein at Millom (iron), Eskdale (iron and granite) and Whitehaven (coal).

Yes, the little **Ravenglass & Eskdale Railway** carried iron ore from 1875 to 1913 and granite from 1922 to 1953. The gauge was narrowed from 3 feet to 1ft 3in during the transition from iron ore to passengers during the Kaiser war. Then when Beckfoot quarry opened a quarter of a mile west of Dalegarth in 1922 the miniature railway gamely carried the granite 4 miles down the line to Murthwaite crushing plant. In 1929 the railway from Murthwaite to the LMSR main line at Ravenglass was laid to dual gauge to give standard-gauge wagons and locomotives access to the crushing plant for railway ballast. That 3-mile section of joint standard gauge and miniature trains was most unusual.

The **Cumberland coalfield** lay under the coastal area around Whitehaven, Workington and Maryport, and galleries extended up to 5 miles under the sea bed. Mining in this area dated from the 17th century. There were more than 70 pits around Whitehaven at one time, though many of them were small. Eight collieries were still at work there in 1950, but seven of them closed from 1955 to 1968. **Haig Colliery** was the last in the Cumberland coalfield; it employed about 1,800 men in its heyday in the 1960s and only closed in 1986 as a result of a geological fault at the coal face and the effects of the national miners' strike of 1984-85. The National Coal Board railways at Haig Colliery and on Whitehaven harbour closed in 1975, being replaced by lorries.

The pithead, screening plant and railway yard were on top of the cliffs above the harbour, and the coal wagons had to be cable-hauled up and down a 1 in 5 incline between the colliery and the harbour. **Whitehaven harbour** opened in 1634 to ship Cumberland coal to Ireland and developed in the 18th century into the third busiest port in Britain after London and Liverpool, exporting Cumberland's natural resources of coal, iron ore, lime and gypsum, and importing tobacco, sugar and rum. More than 1,000 wooden sailing ships were built at Whitehaven and at one time 448 ships were registered there.

The Brocklebank shipping line was founded there in 1785 and moved to Liverpool in 1819. The last coal shipment left in 1982 but coal lorries from Haig Colliery still served BR sidings till the colliery closed in 1986.

Our picture of a coal shipment in Whitehaven harbour shows the giant silos and conveyor built in 1963 to unload phosphate rock from Morocco for the Marchon chemical works and detergent powder factory. Marchon moved to Whitehaven in 1941 and continued to expand till 1989, when it was said to be the largest chemical plant in Western Europe and employed 3,000 people. The company had its own fleet of three ships on the Morocco run. Commercial use of Whitehaven harbour ended in 1992 when Marchon ceased to import rock and the silos and conveyor were demolished. The factory, which aroused environmental opposition over dust, fumes and soap suds in the air and heavy metal pollution of the sea, closed down progressively in 2000-05. Meanwhile the harbour was transformed from commercial to leisure use in the 1990s and now has a 200-berth marina for pleasure craft and a small fishing fleet. The industrial buildings have been replaced by flats, shops and a museum of west Cumberland's industrial and maritime past. Such

is the story of Britain – the shift from industry to leisure – in the second half of the 20th century.

From Cumberland our itinerary then samples the colliery railways of County Durham before terminating this tour of the north country in Northumberland, a relatively sparsely populated, unspoilt, rural county with its population concentrated in the south-east corner. On the Northumberland bank of the River Tyne, **Newcastle** was blackened with smoke from the industries, shipping and railways as the city was developed on coal exports, shipbuilding and every kind of heavy engineering in the 19th century, when it was known as 'The anvil of Europe'. These industries are now defunct, Newcastle is a clean air zone and the city was transformed by modernisation in the second half of the 20th century. The classical city centre built by Dobson and Grainger in 1825-40 has been well preserved and cleaned up to show the ochre colour of the stonework, but the forest of skyscrapers that surround it make Gateshead (County Durham) and Newcastle unrecognisable to anyone who last saw Tyneside in the 1950s.

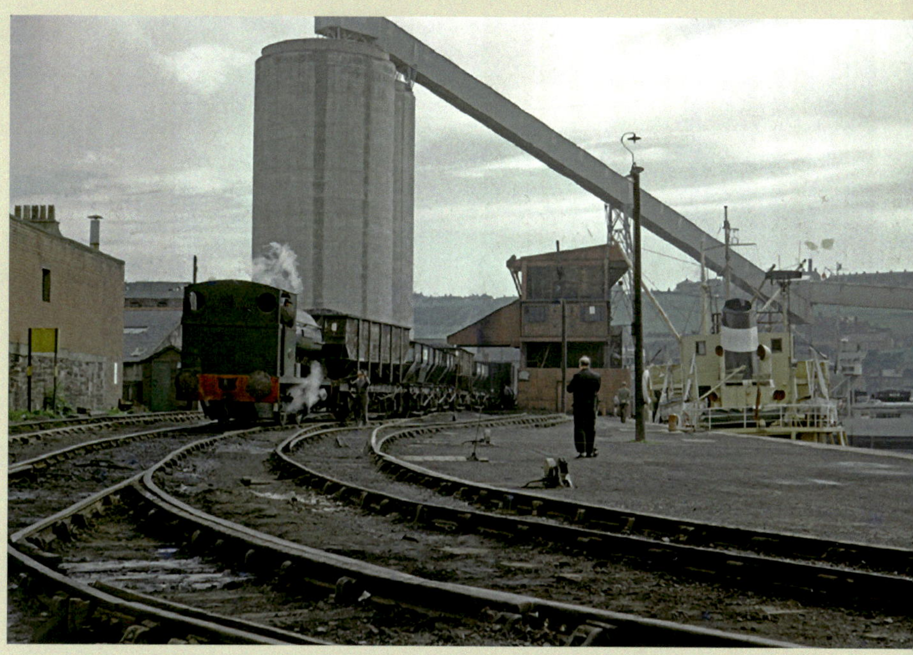

WHITEHAVEN Coal from Haig Colliery is loaded into the hold of a coastal collier from an NCB train in Whitehaven harbour on 19 June 1969. The locomotive *Victoria*, a 1942 Peckett, is being uncoupled from the train by a shunter to go and shunt the BR exchange sidings (off left) and take empty trucks back to the cable incline for reloading at the colliery. The whistles of the harbour engines constantly echoed over the town against the surrounding hills and this was the abiding sound of Whitehaven in the industrial age. The NCB trains at Whitehaven finished in 1975 after being replaced by lorries. The last coal shipment left here in 1982, but the lorries still served the BR coal sidings till Haig Colliery closed in 1986.

The giant silos and conveyor here were built in 1963 to unload phosphate rock from Morocco for the Marchon chemical works and detergent powder factory at Kells. Commercial use of Whitehaven harbour ended in 1992 when Marchon ceased to import rock, and the silos and conveyor were demolished. The factory closed down progressively in 2000-05 because of environmental pollution and the harbour was transformed from commercial to leisure use in the 1990s.

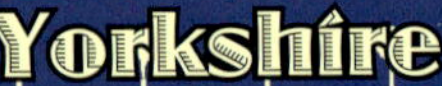

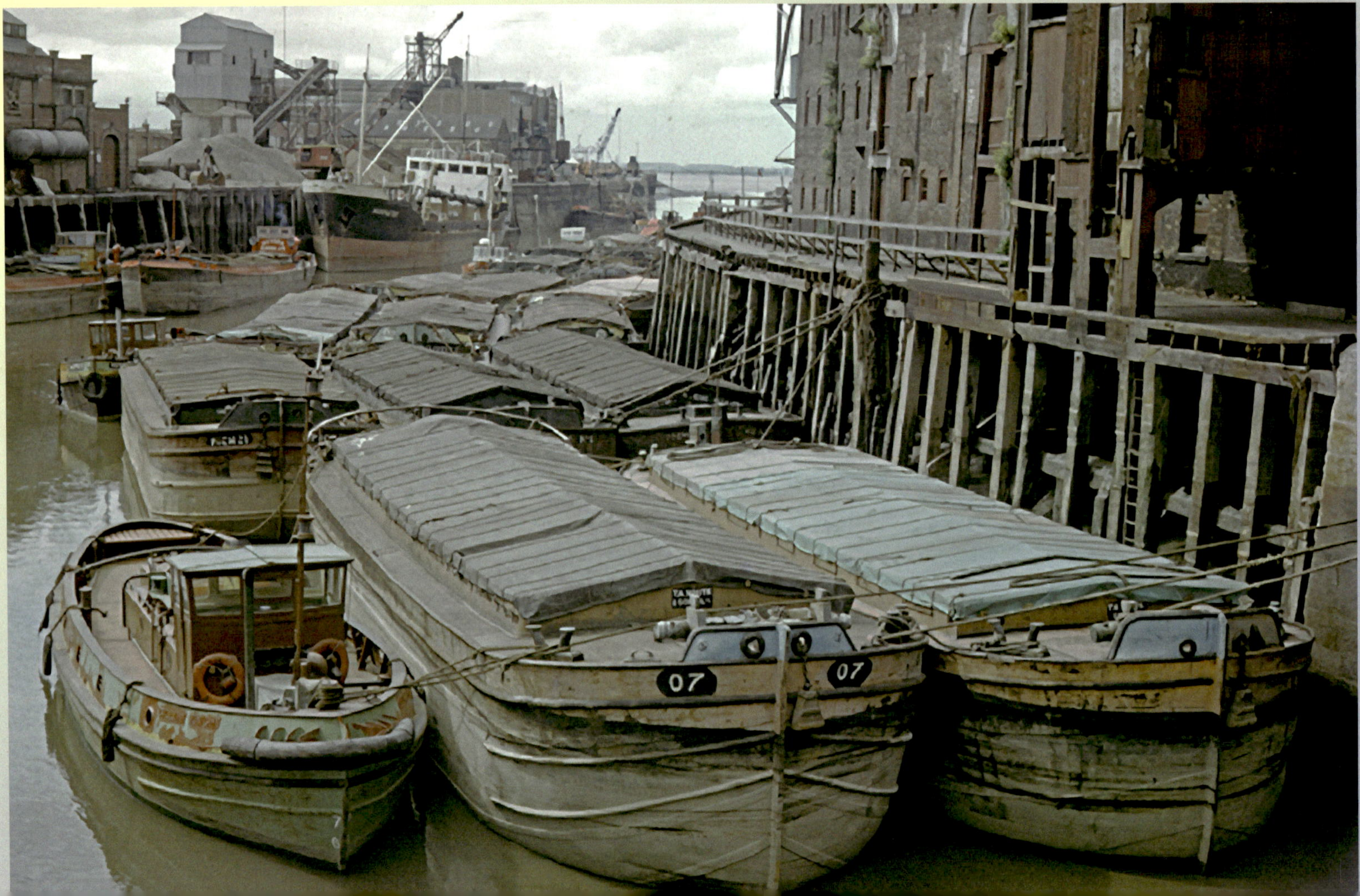

Left: **HULL** Barges, tugs and a coaster lie in the Old Harbour on the River Hull, seen from Drypool Bridge on 16 June 1970 with the Humber estuary in the background. The dumb barges, or lighters, on the right bank are berthed two or three abreast and the motor tugs *Gillian Knight* and *Hippo D* are berthed alongside them on the left. On the left bank of the river are the motor barges *Polar* and *Vega* and the motor coaster *Moderator* beside the gravel crushing plant. These barges navigated the River Hull as far as Beverley with coal, grain and seed, and up and down the Humber tributaries to and from Lincoln, Nottingham, Sheffield, Leeds and York carrying mainly coal, grain and timber. At this time Hull was the third most important port in Britain and the main base for deep-sea fishing.

The Old Harbour is no longer in commercial use, the Trinity House buoys shed (extreme left) is disused, the gravel plant has disappeared, and the factory beyond has been replaced by a hotel. The warehouse on the right has been converted to flats and the only vessel in the Old Harbour today is Hull's last sidewinding trawler *Arctic Corsair*, preserved by the City Council and berthed on the right bank here as a museum of deep-sea fishing. A tidal flood barrier now guards the mouth of the river.

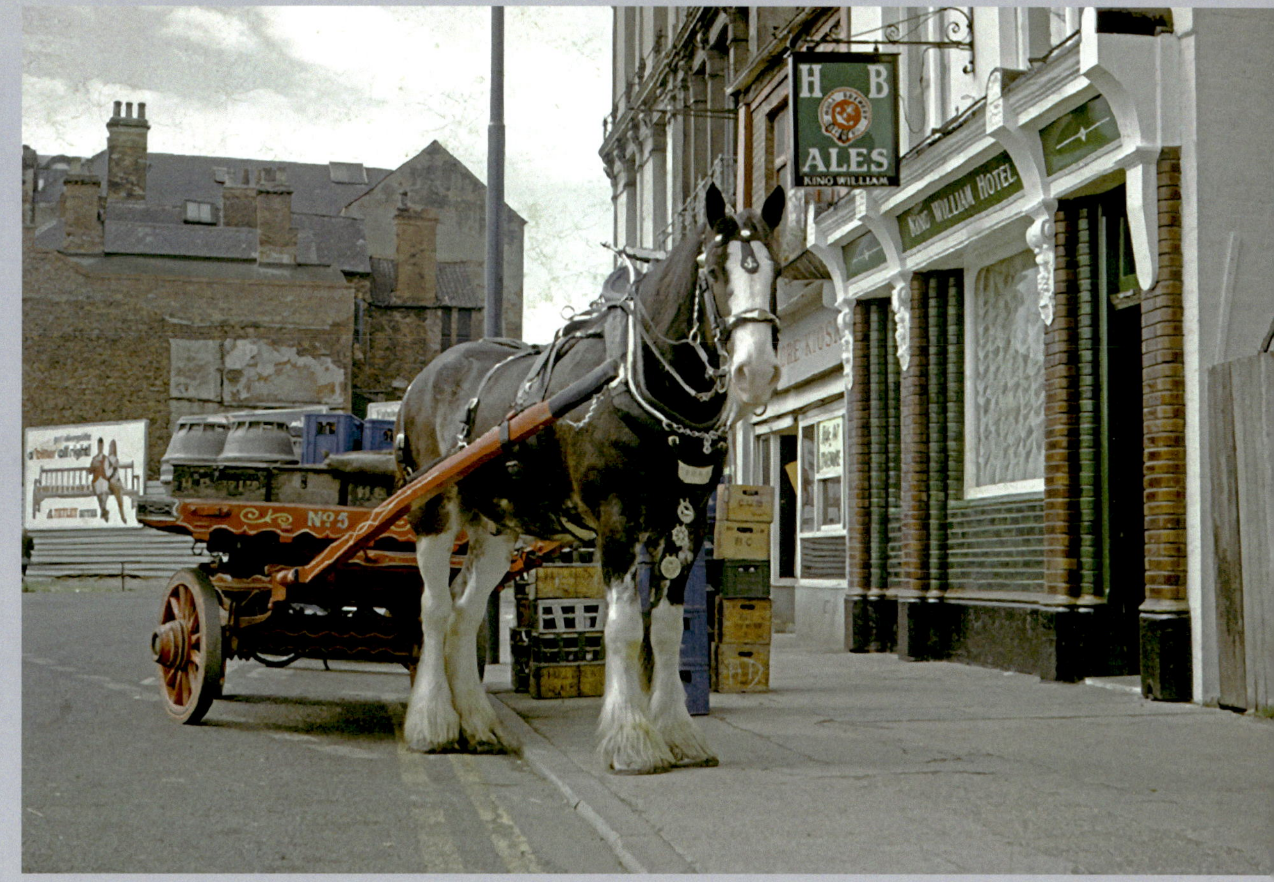

Above: **HULL** Brewery Company's horse dray No 5 is delivering ale at the King William Hotel in Market Place on 16 June 1970. Breweries continued to use four-wheel, flat-bed horse waggons, which they called 'drays', for local deliveries long after all other industries had turned to diesel lorries. Railway companies still had four-wheel horse vans with canvas hoods, or 'tilts', into the early 1950s for collection and delivery of parcels and passengers' trunks. Hull Brewery Company, established in 1888, was taken over by a succession of other companies in 1972, 1985 and 1999. The brewery closed in 2002, when production moved to its latest owners in Wolverhampton.

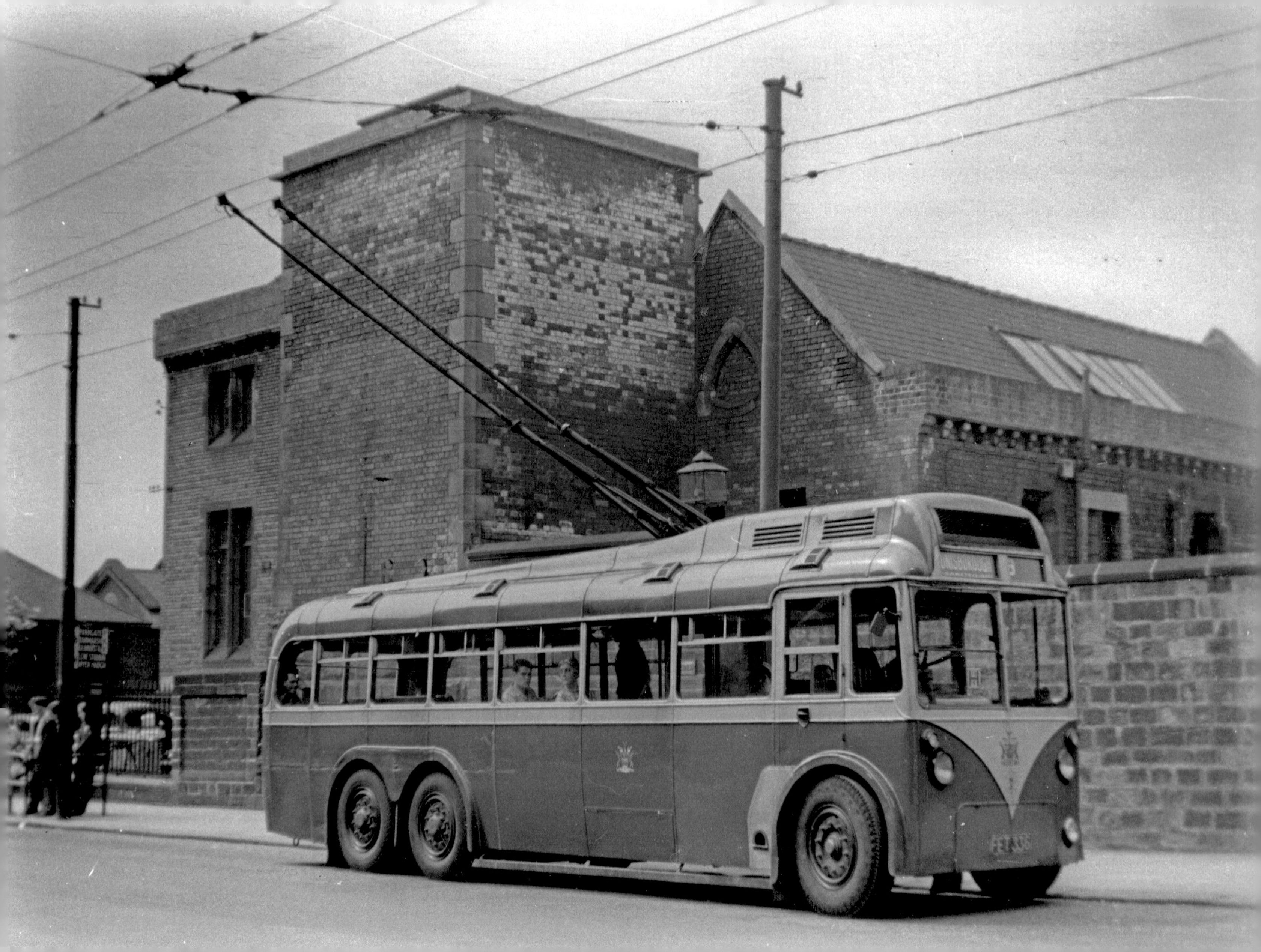

Left: **ROTHERHAM** Single-deck trolleybuses were rare in Britain, but Rotherham was served by two trolleybus systems. The Corporation had an entire fleet of single-deckers from 1912 till 1956, when 14 of these East Lancashire-bodied 38-seaters were rebuilt by Charles Roe of Leeds as 72-seat double-deckers for economies that turned a trading loss into a profit. This bus, No 76 in the fleet, was one of 46 three-axle Daimlers with Crompton Parkinson electric equipment delivered in 1949-50, and one of the 32 vehicles of the batch that were not rebuilt. It is seen on the route to Mexborough and Conisborough on 18 July 1958, a route that was run jointly with Mexborough trolleybuses, also all single-deckers because of low railway bridges. The Mexborough & Swinton Traction Company ceased running trolleybuses in 1961 and Rotherham Corporation followed suit in 1965.

Right: **MEADOWHEAD** was the southern outpost of Sheffield tramways on the A61 road from Chesterfield. A Sheffield Corporation standard tramcar is loading for the route across the city to Sheffield Lane Top in the north on 2 April 1960. This route closed the following day. The car, No 170, was built in 1933-35 with a 61-seat Corporation body on a Peckham truck. Sheffield painted its trams in ivory with dark blue bands. The tram will exit right, where the trolley will be reversed on a triangular arrangement in the overhead wires. Observe the clock on the traction pole.

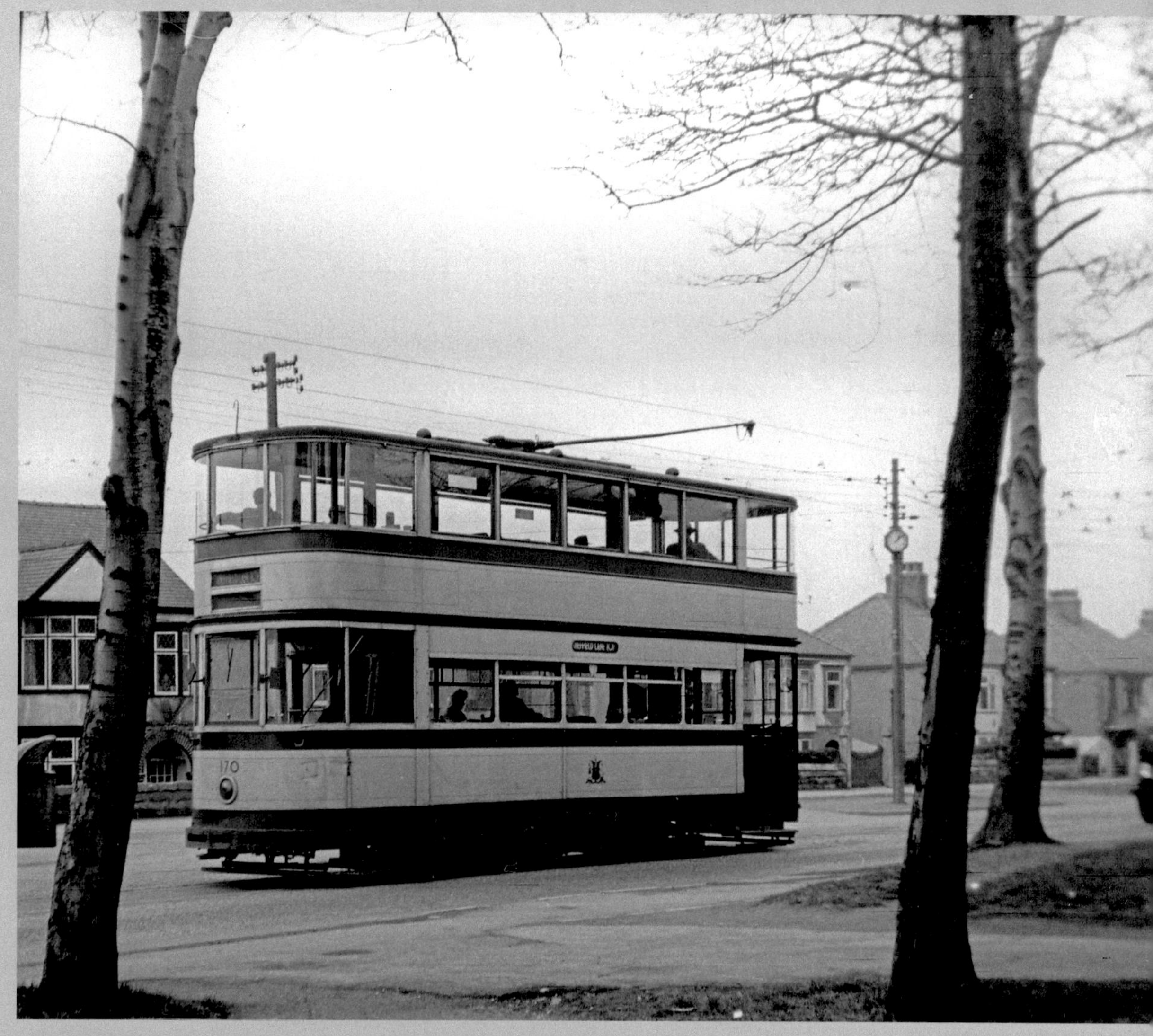

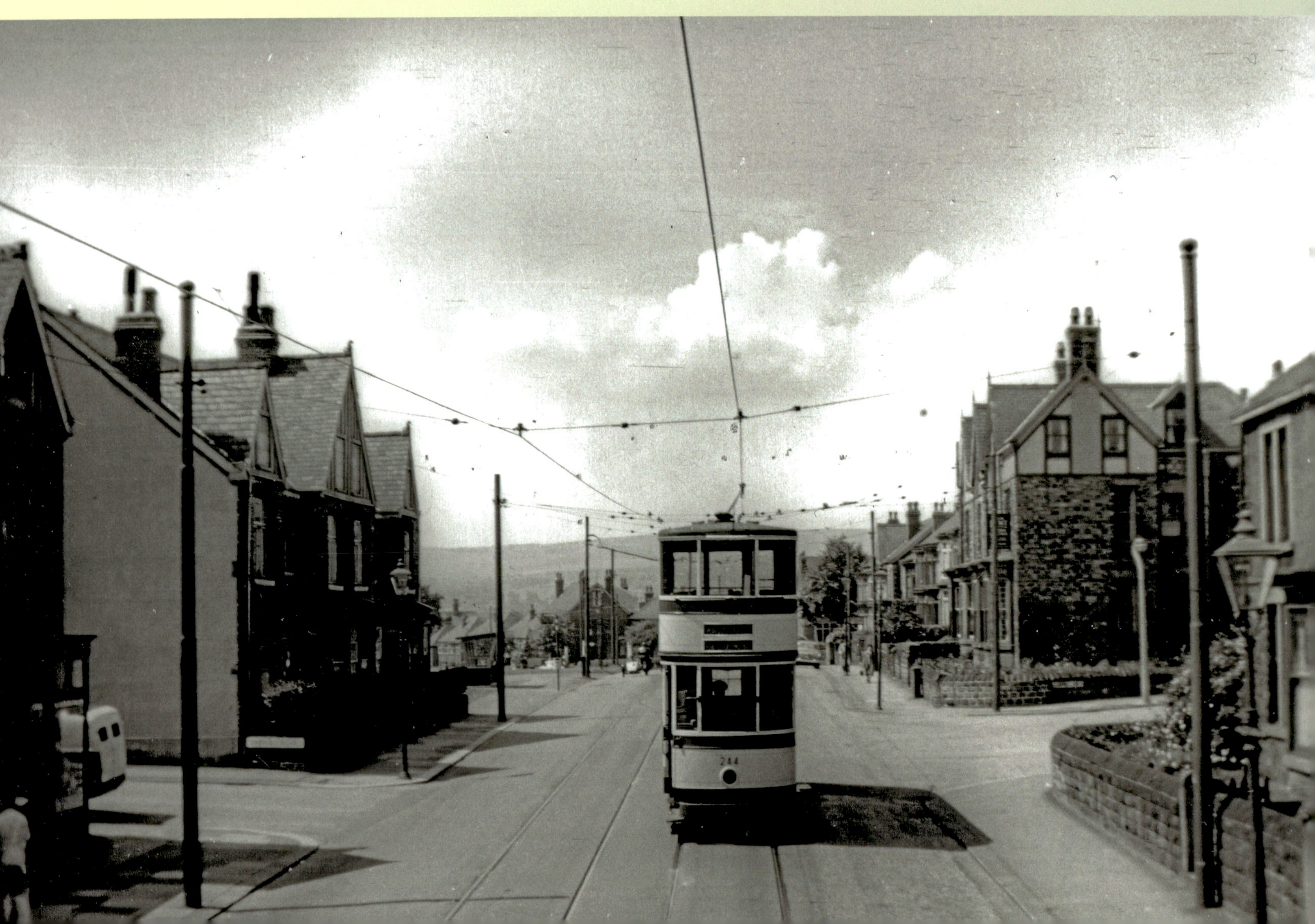

Left: **NORTON WOODSEATS**
The city of Sheffield lies in a hollow on the eastern edge of the High Peak district of Derbyshire. The tramcar, the stone houses, the gas lantern, the tram tracks and the moorland backdrop were characteristic of Pennine industrial towns; only the granite setts are missing as Sheffield had paved many of its tramways in asphalt instead. This tram terminus on Abbey Lane was called WOODSEATS on the tramcar destination blinds and car No 244 of 1936 is seen from the upper saloon of another tramcar leaving the terminus on 17 July 1958. The cross-city route from Woodseats to Wadsley Bridge closed on 3 October 1959.

Right: **NORTON WOODSEATS**
This 69-seat, Roe-bodied Leyland PD3 bus of 1959 looks smart in Sheffield's ivory and dark blue paint scheme without the dark grey roof of earlier Sheffield buses. It is on Abbey Lane at Woodseats tram terminus on 17 July 1958. Route 63 circled around Woodseats and Beauchief and crossed the city centre to terminate at Shirecliffe in the northern suburbs. Tramcar No 161 of 1935 has just arrived at the terminus and passengers are alighting. It is about to reverse over the crossover and the route blinds have already been reset for the return journey to Wadsley Bridge via Shoreham Street. The trolley reverser can be seen in the overhead wires beyond the car. This picture represents the transition from tramcars to motorbuses in Sheffield in 1952-60.

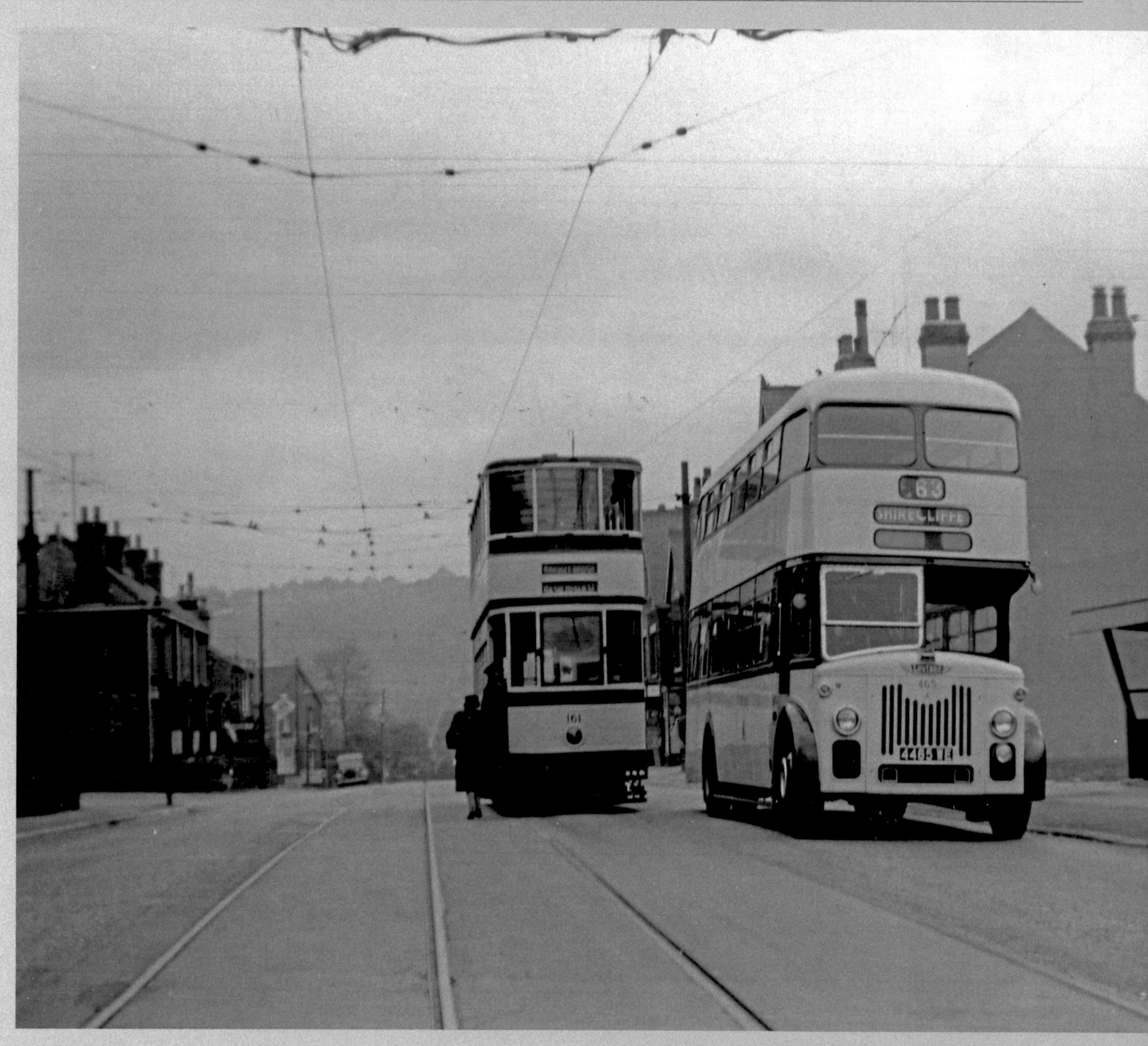

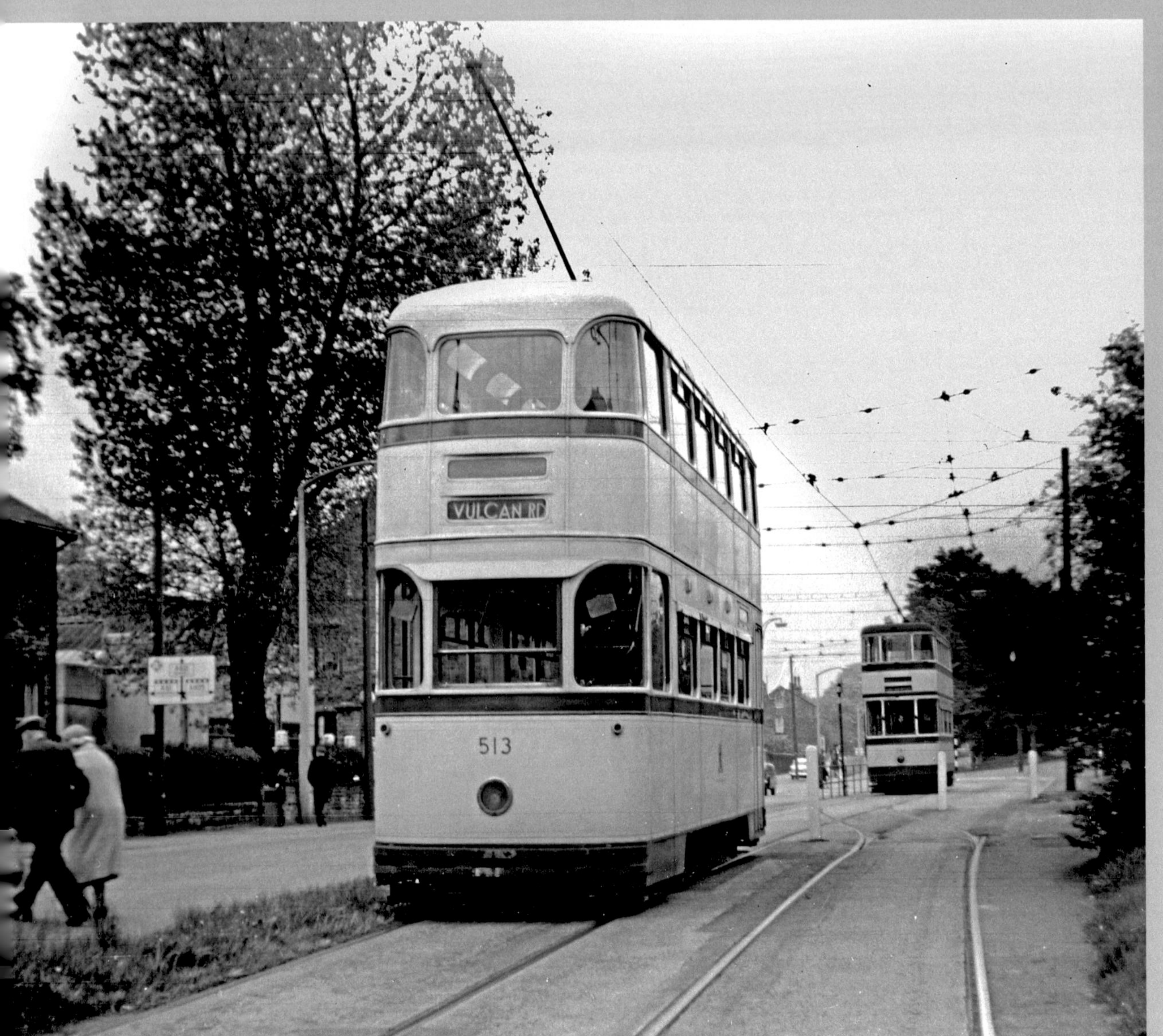

Left: **BEAUCHIEF** Two more modern classes of tramcars in Sheffield are seen on the reservation alongside Abbeydale Road South at Beauchief terminus on 19 May 1959. Car No 513 was one of 35 built by Charles Roberts of Wakefield in 1950-52 to match the Corporation's prototype of 1946. The tramcar in the background is one of 81 rather trim standard cars with slightly arched roofs, built by the Corporation in 1936-44.

Right: **SHEFFIELD** Kerbside loading at the Town Hall takes place on a three-track section of the tramway in Pinstone Street on 2 April 1960. Car No 68 is a standard 61-seater of 1930 built by the Corporation on a Peckham truck. The centre track was used by cars on another route that stopped elsewhere. It was unusual to see tramcars loading at the kerb in Britain, although there was no reason why the track should not loop into the kerbside as it does here. Some systems built passenger loading islands in the middle of the road. The Town Hall, with its 180-foot clock tower, was built in 1891-96 to a design by Edward Mountford.

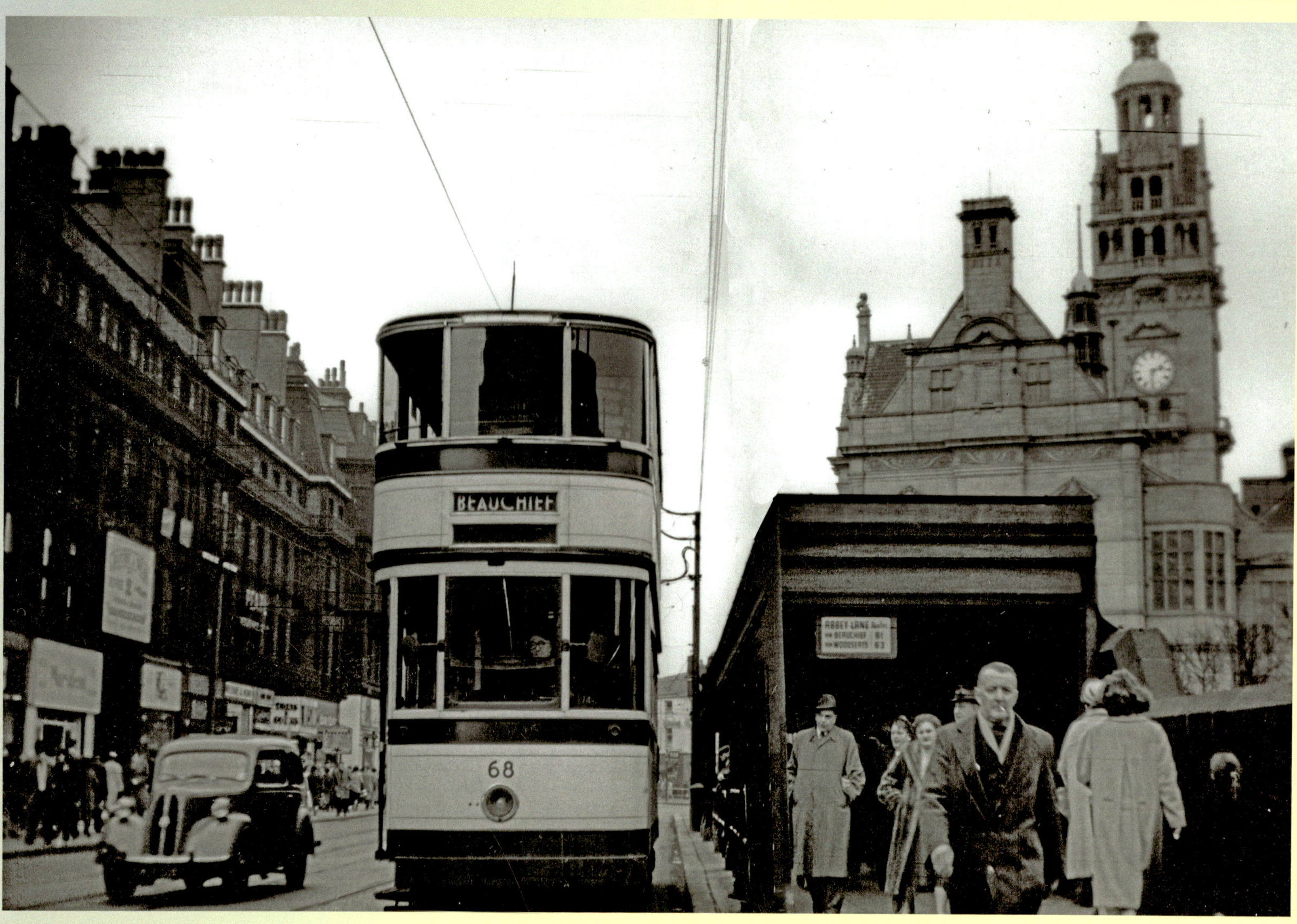
BEAUCHIEF
68
ABBEY LANE
VIA BEAUCHIEF | 81
VIA WOODSEATS | 63

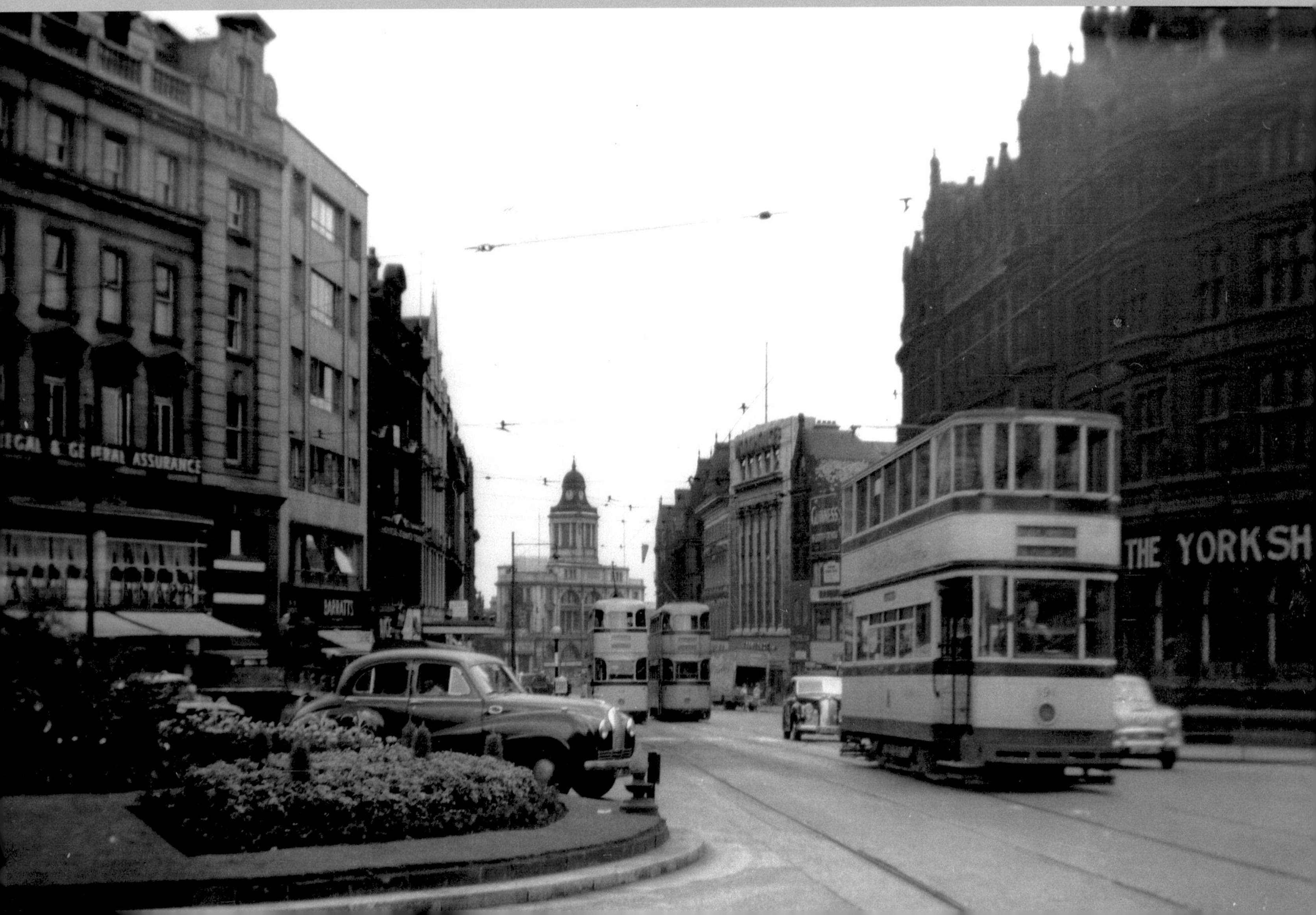

Left: **SHEFFIELD** Even in the eighth year of Sheffield's tramway scrapping programme, tramcars still dominated the city centre. In this view of Fargate on 19 May 1959 are three tramcars and three private cars. A 1948 Austin A70 is pulling out of Leopold Street and tramcar No 191 of 1934 is being tailed by a 1948 Austin Princess and flanked on its nearside by a 1955 Standard. Two more modern tramcars of 1950-52 are passing each other halfway down the street. The *Sheffield Telegraph* office terminates the view. Sheffield's last tram ran through Fargate on the route from Vulcan Road to Beauchief on 8 October 1960.

The Yorkshire Penny Bank stands on the corner of Surrey Street (right). It was founded at Leeds in 1859 as a savings bank for 'the working men of the West Riding' and branches extended through midland and northern England. The 'penny' dropped from the name in 1959. Fargate is now a pedestrian precinct with restricted access for loading vehicles.

Right: **SHEFFIELD** The clean outlines of Sheffield Corporation's standard trams were complemented by their smart, ivory paintwork, trimmed with dark blue bands and simple but neat ochre lining-out of the panels, the city coat of arms and no lettering or advertising. Standard car No 161 of 1933 is loading at the island stone shelter in Fitzalan Square on its way from Woodseats to Wadsley Bridge on 19 May 1959. This route closed on 3 October that year. The standard trams had six route screens: a destination and 'via' screen at each end and a destination screen on each side.

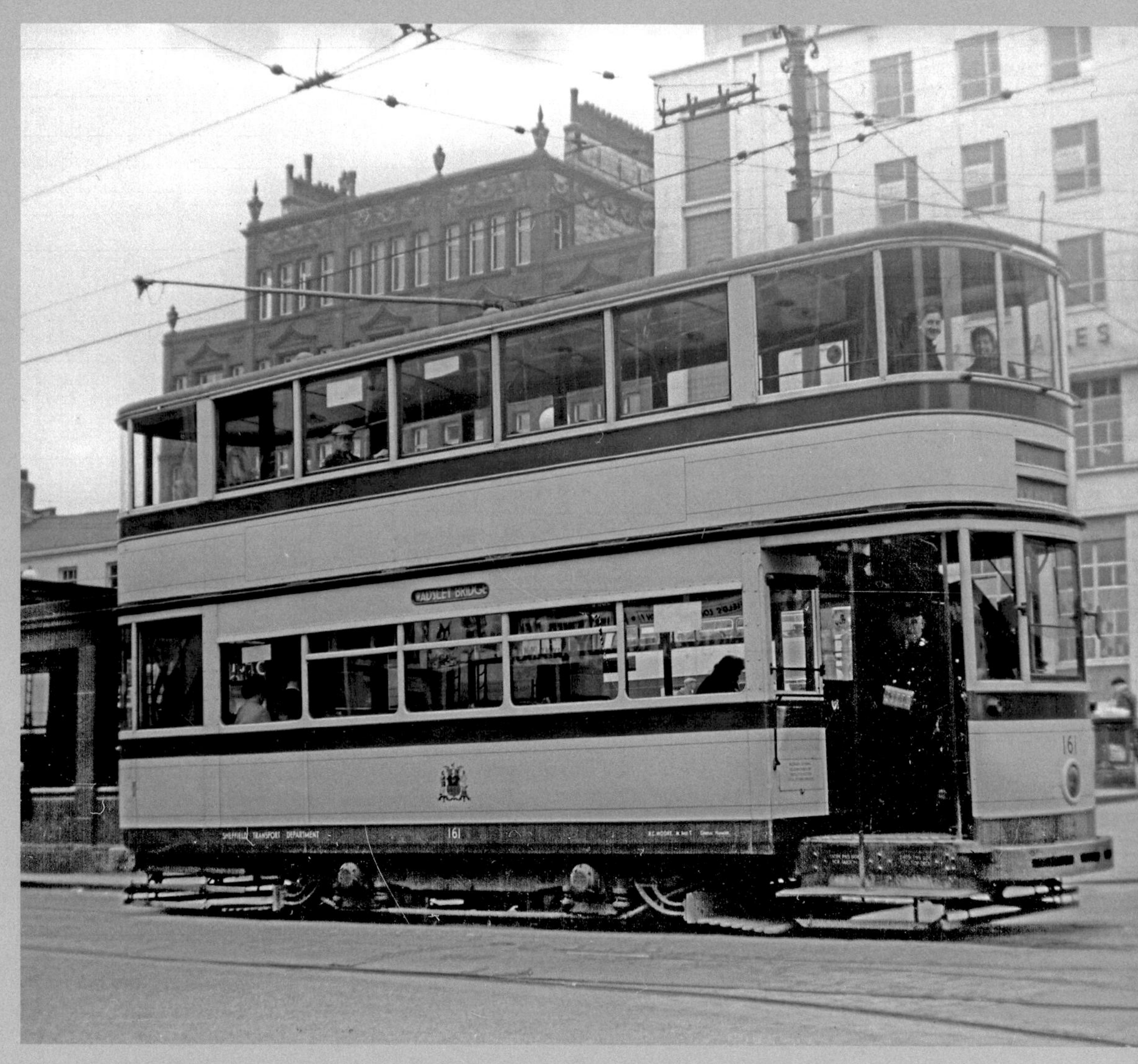

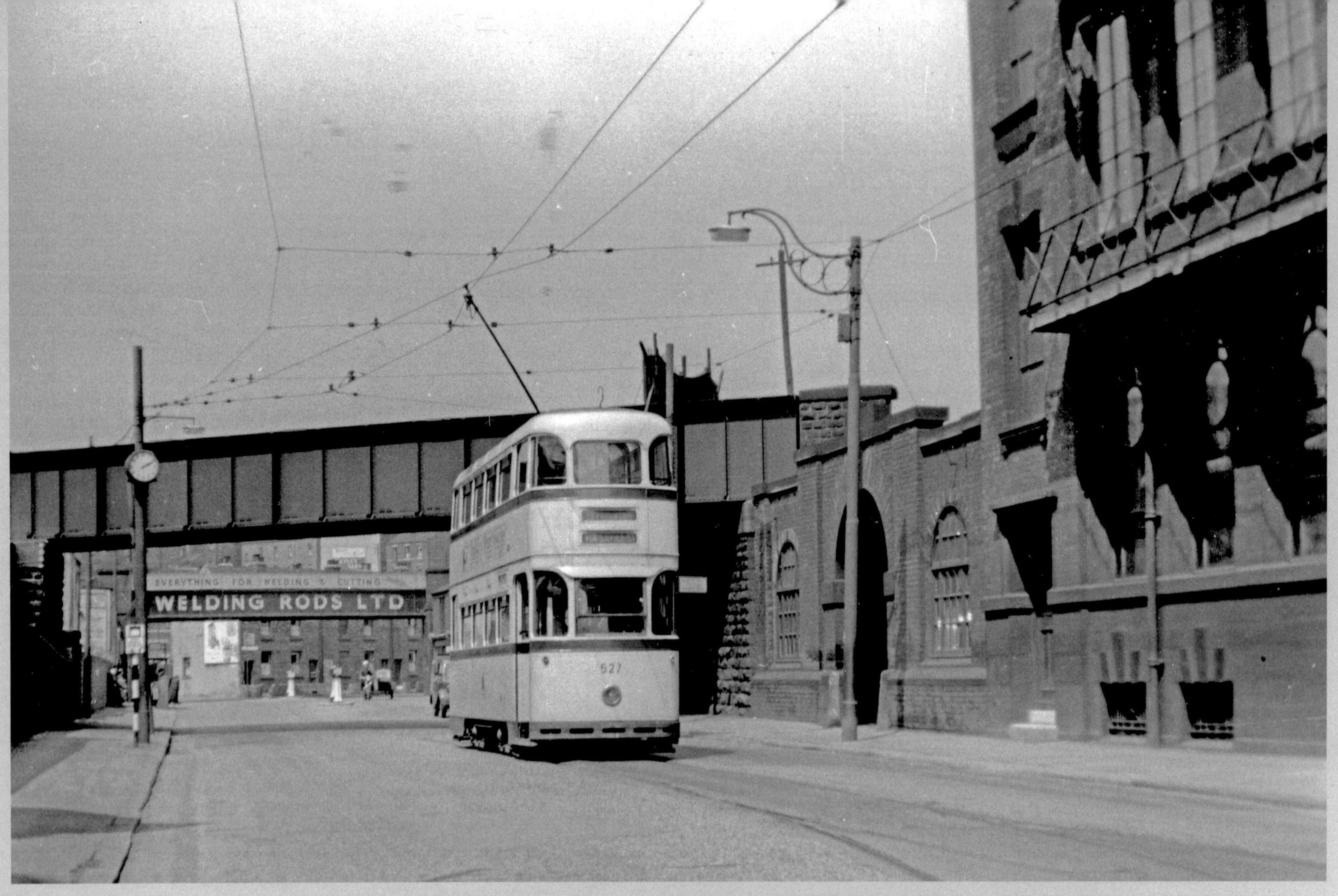

BRIGHTSIDE was the ironically named tram terminus among the grim, industrial steel works along the Don valley north-east of the city, but on this day, 17 July 1958, it looks brighter in the presence of a shiny, ivory tramcar glinting in the sunlight. Car 527 was one of the 36 post-war tramcars of this type, all with 62 seats, built by Charles Roberts on Maley & Taunton trucks. The last of these cars were delivered after the Corporation had decided to replace the trams with buses and they were prematurely scrapped after a minimum of only eight years, in contrast to the 30 years of some of the other cars still in service.

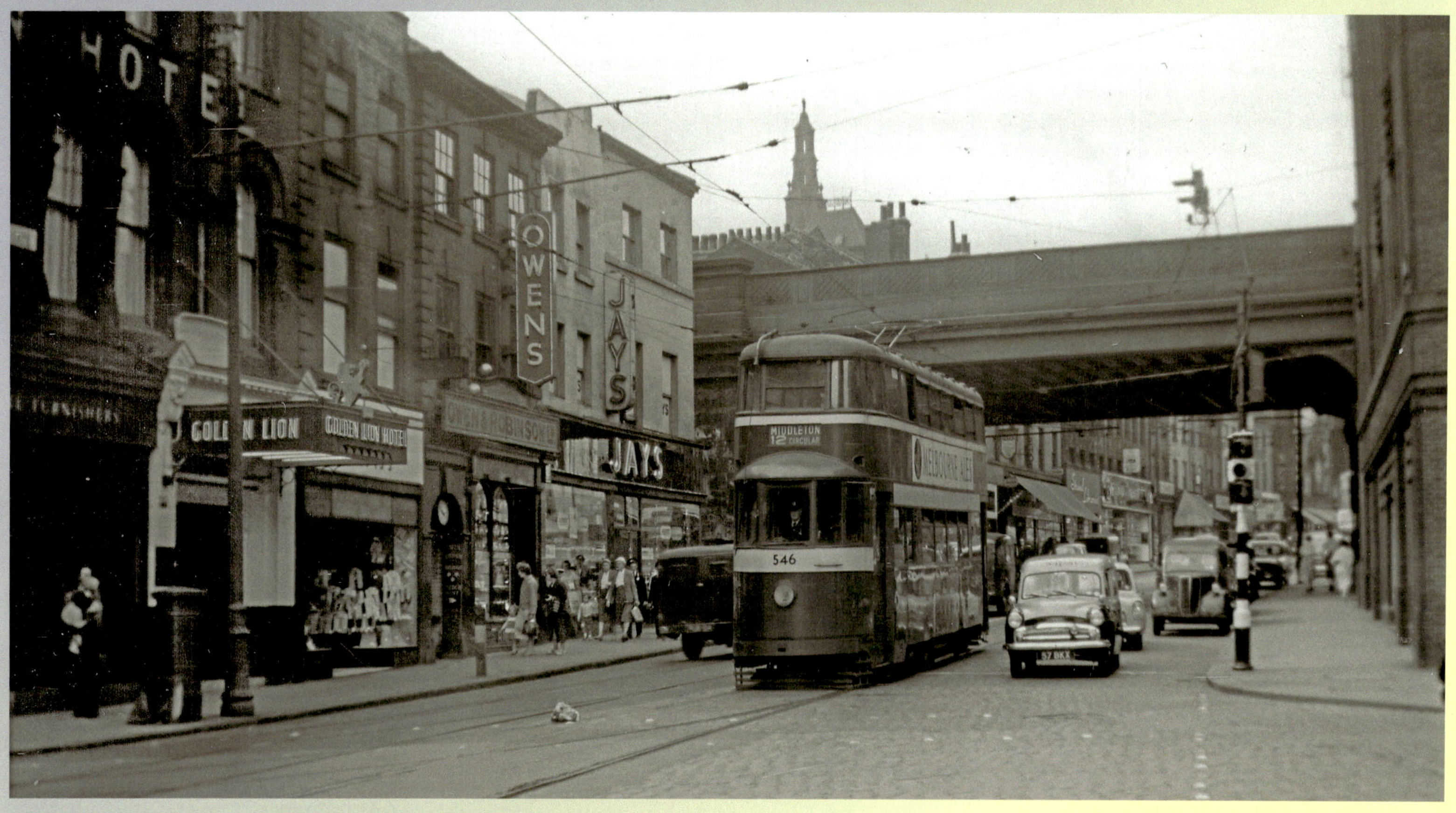

LEEDS trams were augmented by these second-hand 'Feltham' class cars from London Transport for the last 10 years of the system. A total of 90 'Felthams' arrived in Leeds in 1950-52 although only 83 were adapted for service there. These large, speedy cars with centre entrances were contemporaries of the 'Horsfield' standards, having been built in 1930-31, but while the 'Horsfield' car was a standard 60-seat four-wheeler, the 'Feltham' was a high-powered bogie car with 70 seats in sumptuously furnished and heated saloons, and gave a smooth, steady ride, although they were heavy on the tracks. They were built by the Union Construction Company at Feltham on EMB bogies for London United Tramways and Metropolitan Electric Tramways, and were inherited by LT in 1933. On its outward, clockwise journey around the Middleton circular route south of the city on the last day of service, 28 March 1959, car No 546 drifts down Lower Briggate under the railway bridge just east of Leeds City station and pauses at the signals at the junction with Swinegate (left) and the line to Swinegate car sheds and workshops.

LEEDS Kirkgate was the city terminus of the last two tram routes. A Leeds 'Horsfield' car and an ex-London 'Feltham' car, both of 1931, are on lay-over in Kirkgate on 19 September 1959, less than two months before closure. The Corn Exchange was nominally the city terminus, but for the last eight months of operation the trams were relegated to this single-line loop around the block east of the exchange. The trams unloaded and took their lay-over here, then followed the granite-paved turnout into New York Street to reload there. Kirkgate leads to the parish church of St Peter, towering in the background, and the bridge carried the former NER line east to Hull and York. The 'Horsfield' car is operating route 22 to Temple Newsam and the 'Feltham' is on route 18 to Cross Gates, both east of the city. Two Leeds Corporation buses, both Roe-bodied Leylands, can be seen behind the trams. Leeds buses and trams were previously blue and cream, but from 1950 the trams were repainted crimson and cream and the buses two-tone green.

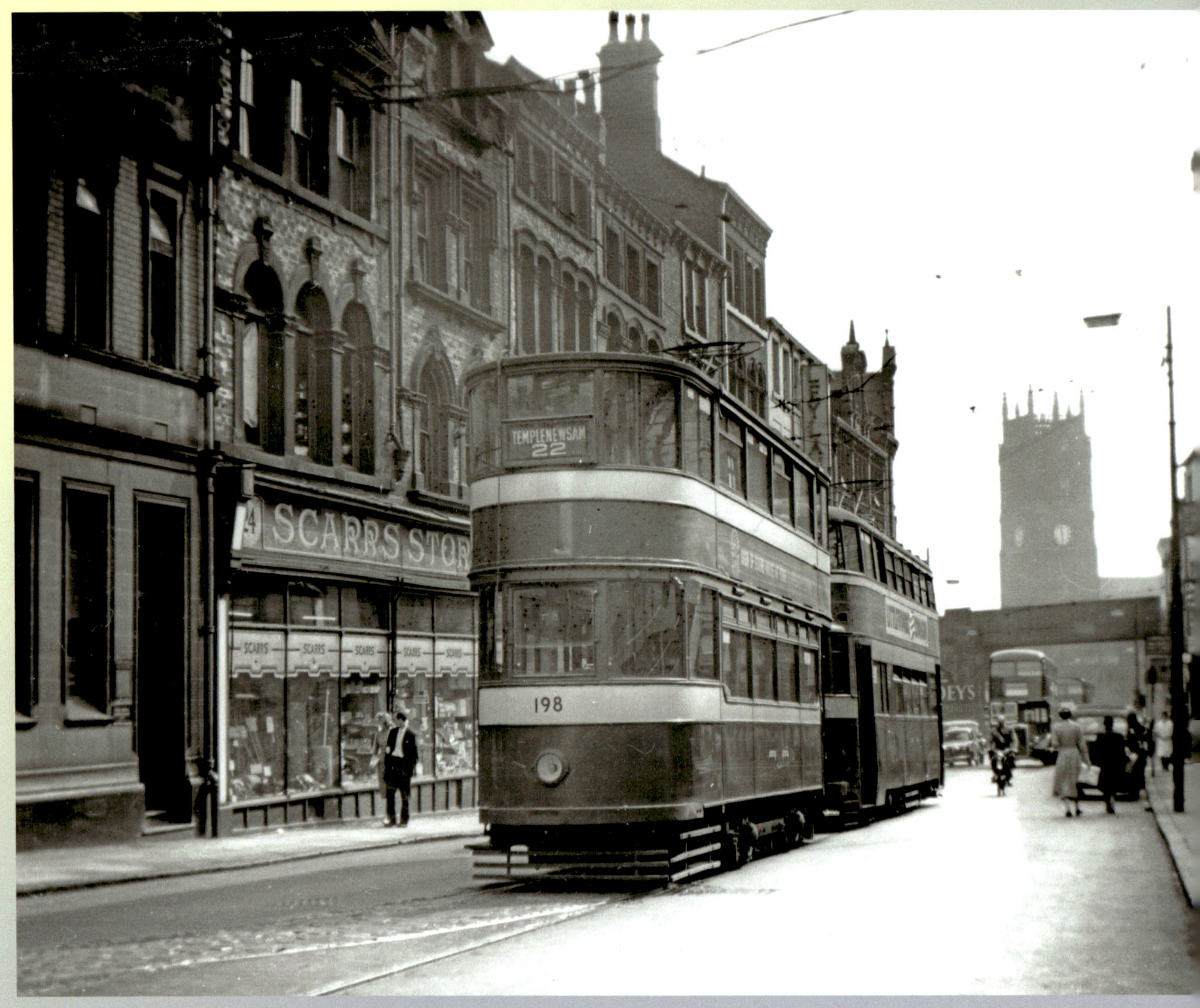

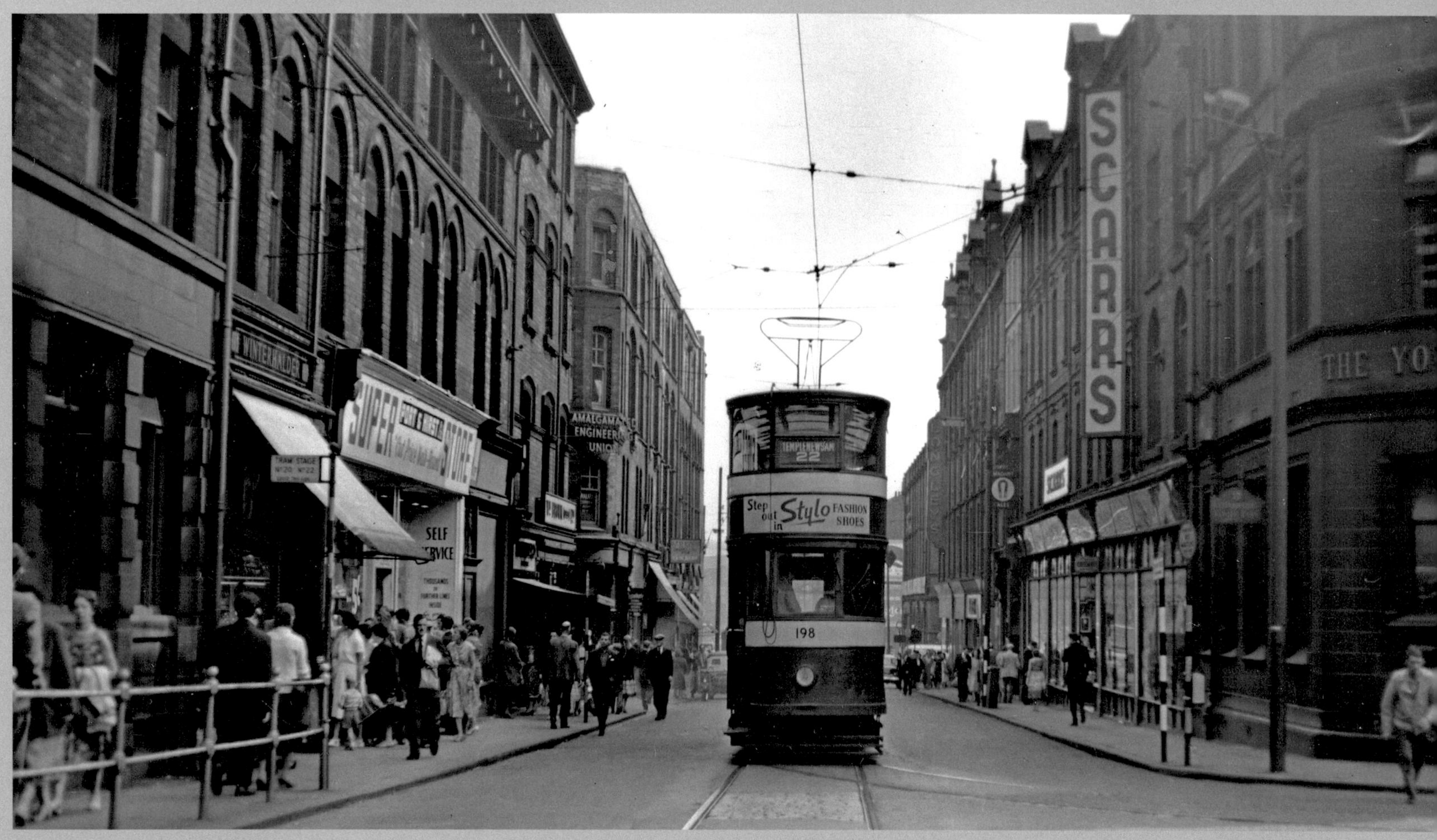

LEEDS A reflex right turn out of Kirkgate brought the trams into New York Street, where 'Horsfield' car No 198 loads at the stop flag on the left, framed between the grimy, four-storey buildings as it sets forth on its run east to Temple Newsam on 19 September 1959. New York Street, York Street and York Road carried the last two tram routes out of the city, dividing at Halton Dial for Cross Gates and Temple Newsam. The Yorkshire Penny Bank, which was founded in Leeds in 1859, is on the right, and next door is the other side of Scarr's department store, which we saw opposite in Kirkgate.

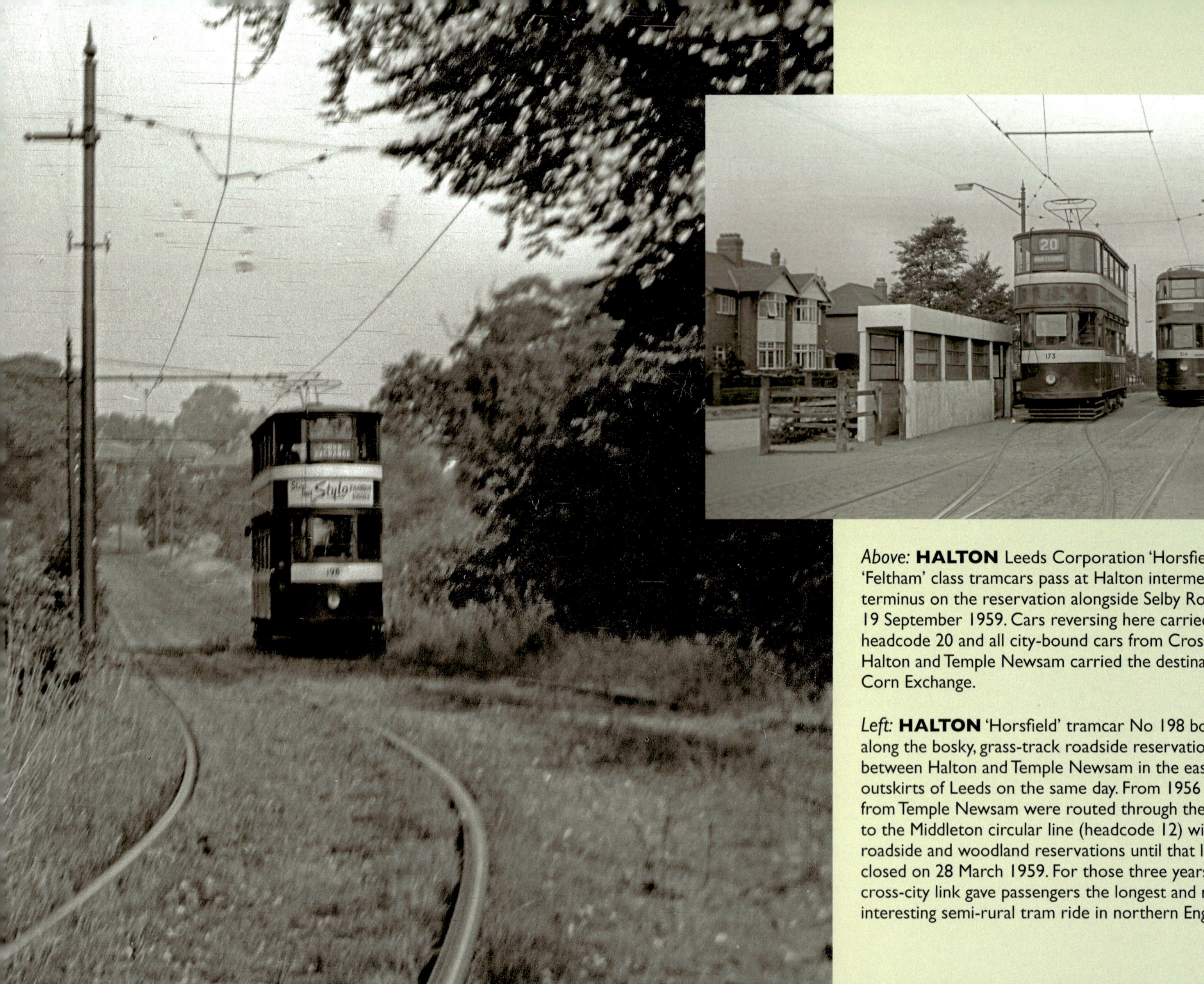

Above: **HALTON** Leeds Corporation 'Horsfield' and 'Feltham' class tramcars pass at Halton intermediate terminus on the reservation alongside Selby Road on 19 September 1959. Cars reversing here carried the headcode 20 and all city-bound cars from Cross Gates, Halton and Temple Newsam carried the destination Corn Exchange.

Left: **HALTON** 'Horsfield' tramcar No 198 bowls along the bosky, grass-track roadside reservation between Halton and Temple Newsam in the eastern outskirts of Leeds on the same day. From 1956 cars from Temple Newsam were routed through the city to the Middleton circular line (headcode 12) with its roadside and woodland reservations until that line closed on 28 March 1959. For those three years that cross-city link gave passengers the longest and most interesting semi-rural tram ride in northern England.

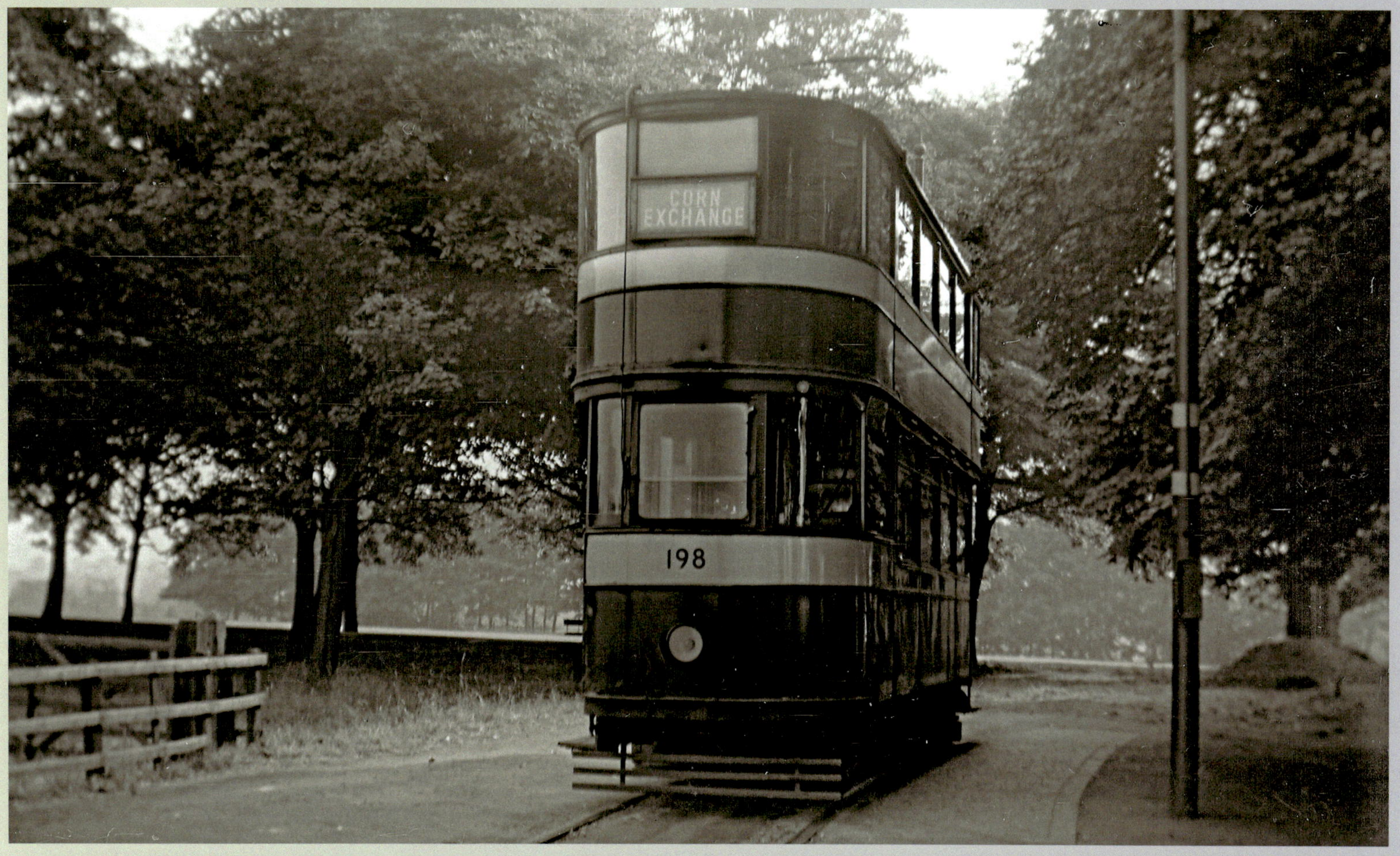

TEMPLE NEWSAM The end of the line: 'Horsfield' tramcar No 198, built by Brush in 1931, stands at the bucolic terminus on the edge of the woods at Temple Newsam (headcode 22) on 19 September 1959. This was on the edge of Temple Newsam Park, with gardens and golf courses surrounding Temple Newsam House, a 16th-, 17th- and 18th-century mansion with one of the finest collections of paintings, furniture and porcelain in Britain. The Temple Newsam and Cross Gates lines were the last two tramways in Leeds and closed together on 7 November 1959.

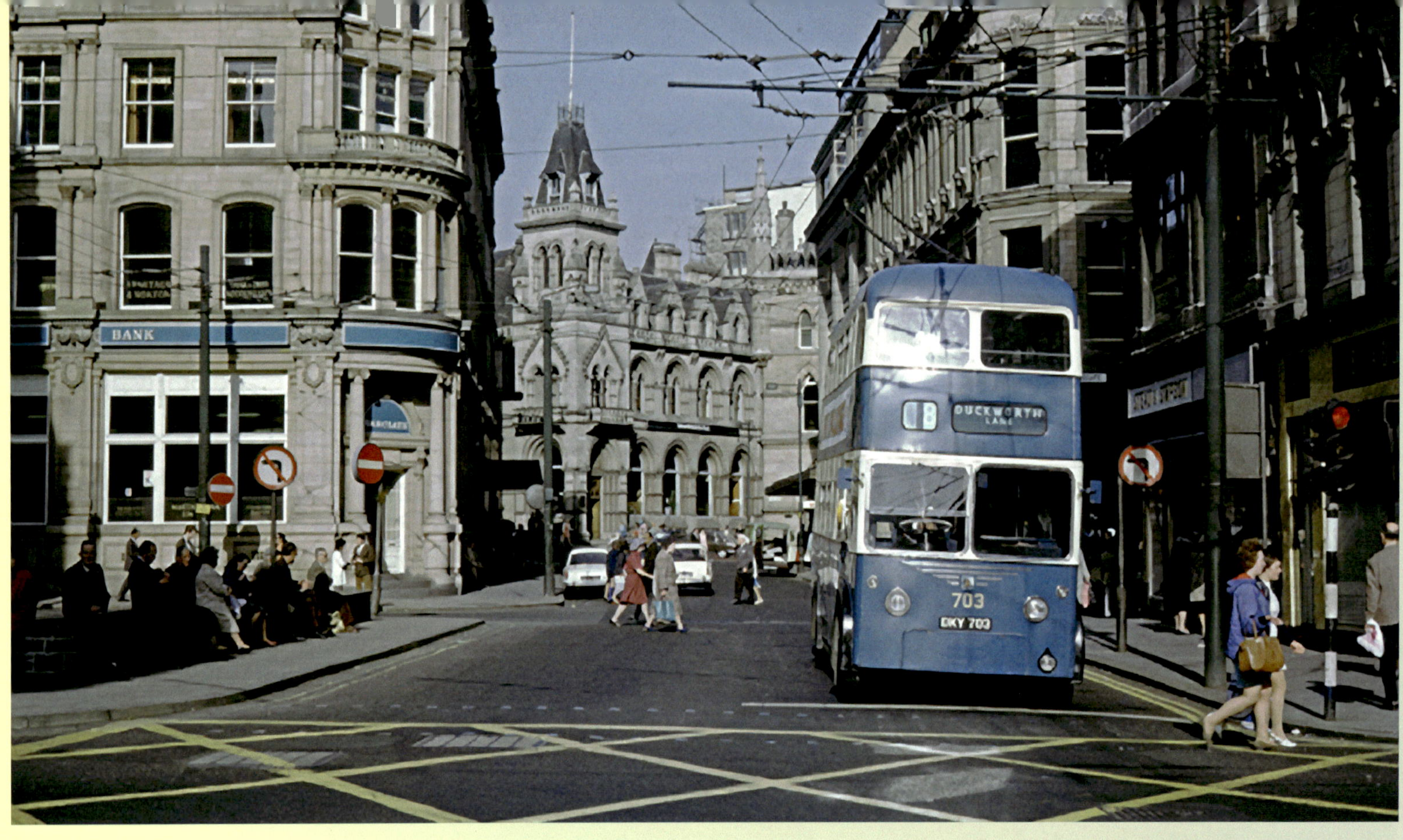

BRADFORD and Leeds shared the distinction of running the first trolleybus services in Britain in 1911. While Leeds abandoned trolleybuses in 1928, Bradford, with its steep hills, retained an extensive system. The last new trolleybus arrived in 1963 and Bradford went on to run Britain's last trolleybuses in 1972. As other trolleybus systems closed down Bradford collected an eclectic fleet of second-hand vehicles from Southend, Notts & Derby, Llanelly, Darlington, St Helens, Brighton, Hastings, Doncaster and Mexborough. The last two routes were the east-west route 7 from Thornbury to Thornton and the 8 from the city centre north-west to Duckworth Lane, where the last working trolleybus depot was sited. Route 8 started here in the commercial heart of the city on a loop around this square in Tyrrel Street, and here we see No 703 waiting for the green signal to turn right into Sunbridge Road on 5 October 1971. It has a 1959 East Lancashire body on a 1945 Karrier chassis with Metropolitan Vickers electric equipment. This was the commercial centre of Bradford and the Yorkshire stone buildings in this scene had all been cleaned since the era of steam woollen mills and still stand today, though most of them have changed their original use. This is now a pedestrianised conservation area with flush paving and restricted access for loading vehicles.

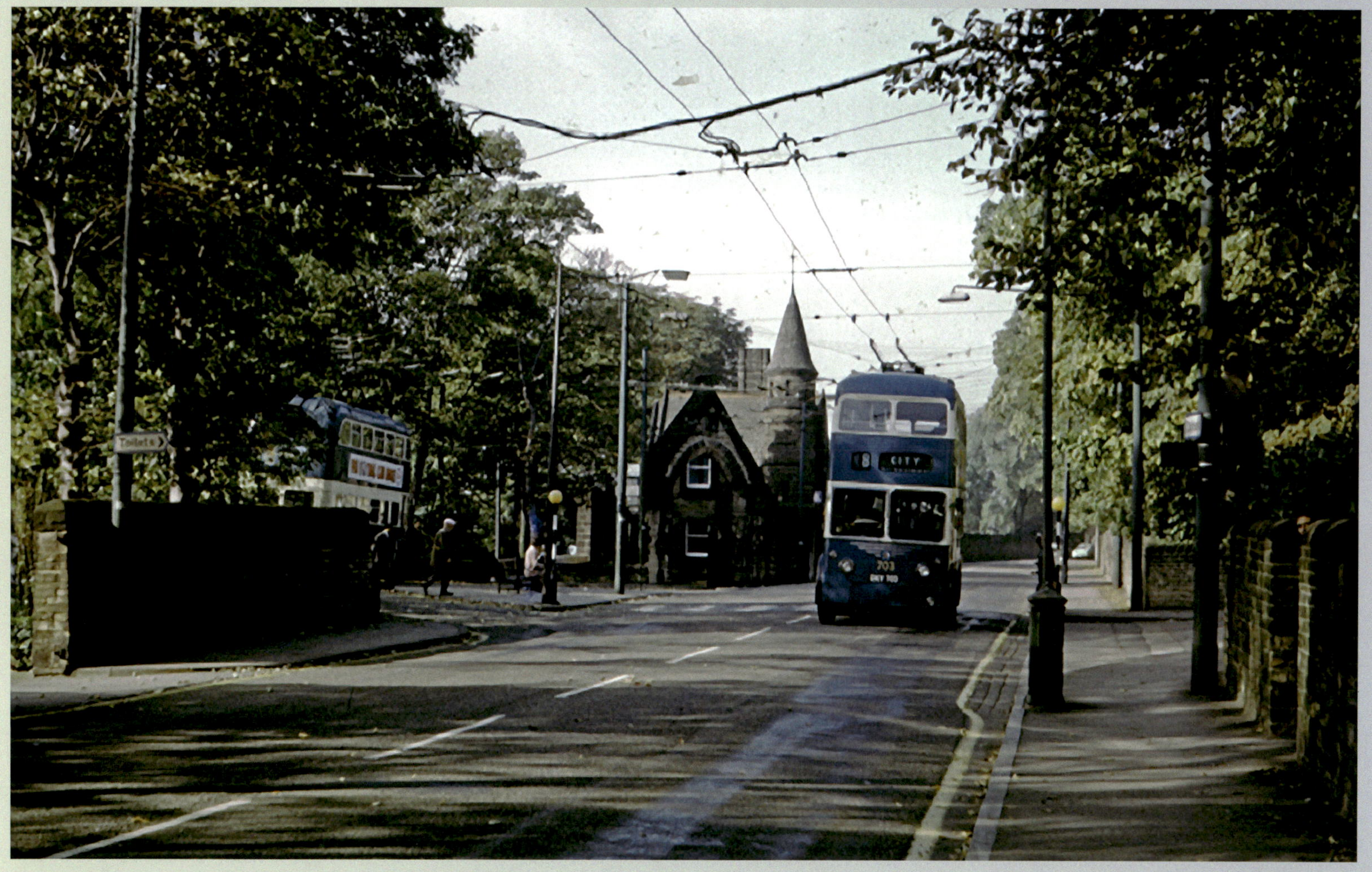

BRADFORD trolleybus No 703 is seen again, leaving Duckworth Lane terminus city-bound on the same day. No 711, of the same type, has taken its place on the terminal loop.

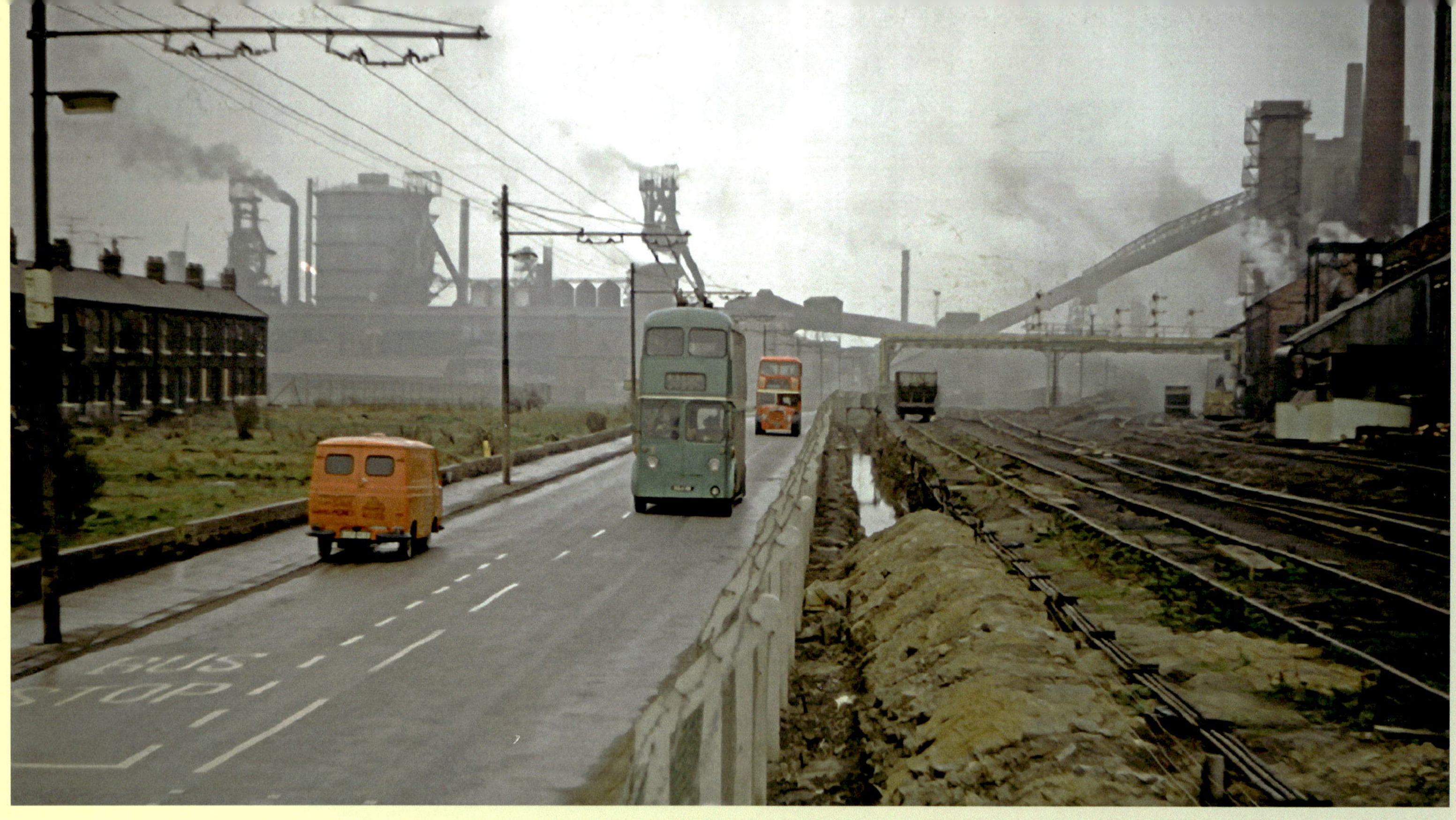

TEESSIDE trolleybuses were promoted in 1912 by the Cleveland Iron & Steel Works to take men to and from the work sites along the south bank of the River Tees near Middlesbrough. The overhead and depot were ready by 1915, but the Kaiser war deferred operations till 1919, when they were run by a joint board of Eston UDC and Middlesbrough Corporation. Roe-bodied Sunbeam trolleybus No 6 of the Teesside Railless Traction Board leads a Bristol Lodekka motorbus of United Automobile Services along Eston Road between South Bank and Grangetown on 28 March 1970. Bolckow Terrace (left) was named after Henry Bolckow, who founded the iron and steel industry on Teesside. The firm of Bolckow, Vaughan, which initiated the trolleybus system, was taken over in 1929 by Dorman, Long, which built the great steel arch bridges at Newcastle in 1928 and Sydney in 1932. The steel works supplied the 550-volt traction current till 1955, when it was switched to the National Grid. The Grangetown route was extended in three stages from 1951 to 1968, linking Grangetown and Normanby via Eston in a loop for circular operation in 1968. This was the last trolleybus extension in Britain. The trolleybuses were repainted from dark green to turquoise when Teesside Borough Transport took over later in 1968. This was Britain's last but one trolleybus system to close down, in 1971, one year before Bradford's.

All the elements of this scene have disappeared: the iron and steel works, the railways serving them, Bolckow Terrace and Eston Road, which has been intercepted by the Grangetown bypass.

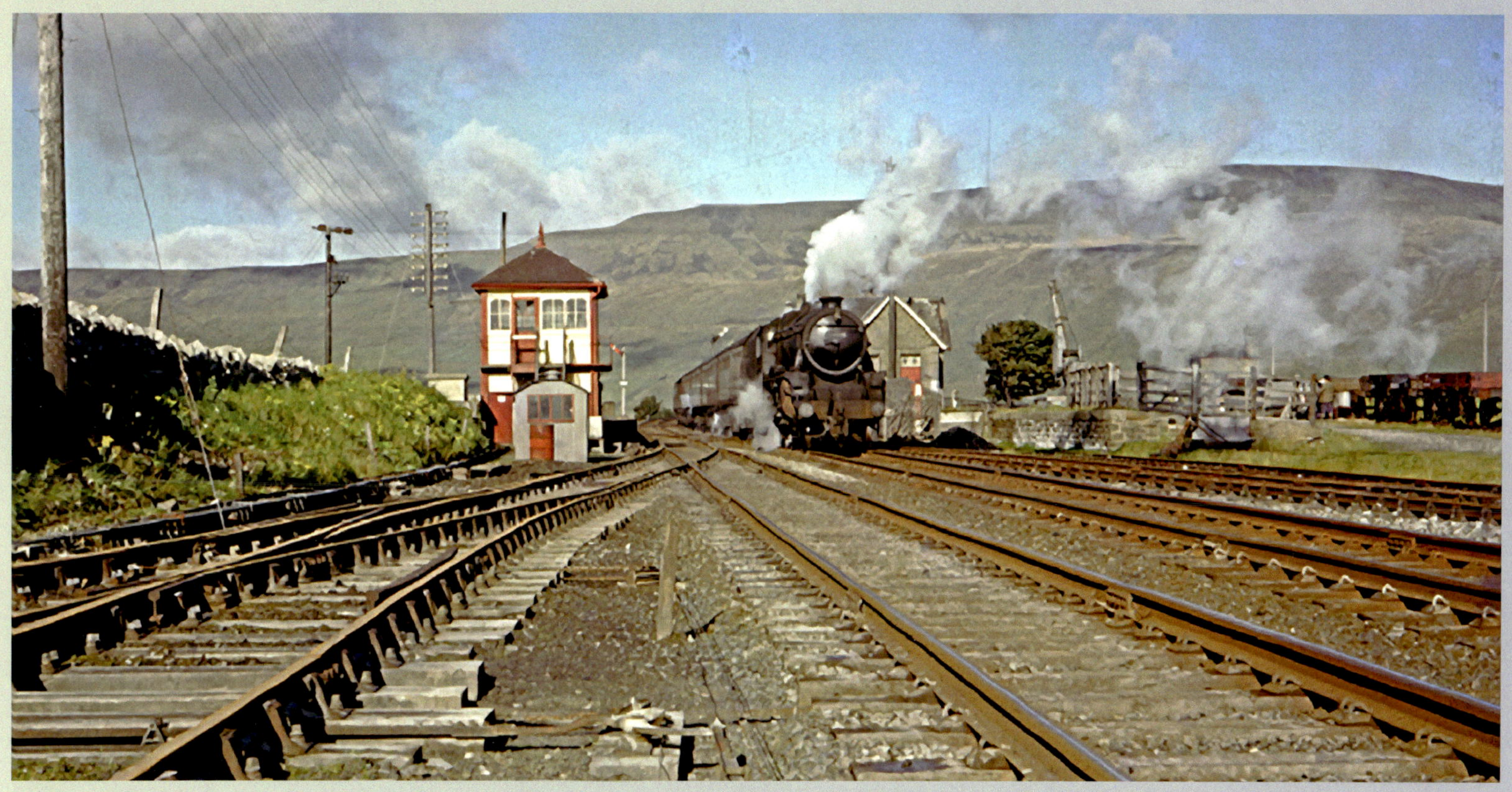

RIBBLEHEAD station at the head of Ribblesdale is 1,025 feet above sea level on the Settle-Carlisle section of the former Midland main line, serving a remote hamlet and farming community. Behind it, Whernside rises to 2,419 feet, the highest peak in Yorkshire. 'Black Five' No 44898, built at Crewe in 1945, has stopped with a Carlisle to Bradford train on 25 September 1963. The station waiting room doubled as a chapel with a harmonium for Sunday services until 1956, the stony station approach road was used as a sheep market, and from 1938 to 1970 the railway station was also the highest weather station in England as the station master and his wife recorded and reported wind speeds and rainfall for the Air Ministry, the RAF and the river authorities for Yorkshire and Lancashire.

The quarry sidings and signal cabin closed in 1969 and the station closed in 1970, but the up platform reopened as a halt for southbound trains in 1986 and a new down platform was built south of the up platform in 1993. This station is now used mainly by fell walkers. The Settle & Carlisle Railway Trust restored the derelict up-side buildings as a Midland Railway period station and visitor centre, which opened in 2000. The former quarry is now a nature reserve and new sidings have been laid opposite the up platform and behind the down platform for the shipment of timber from nearby plantations.

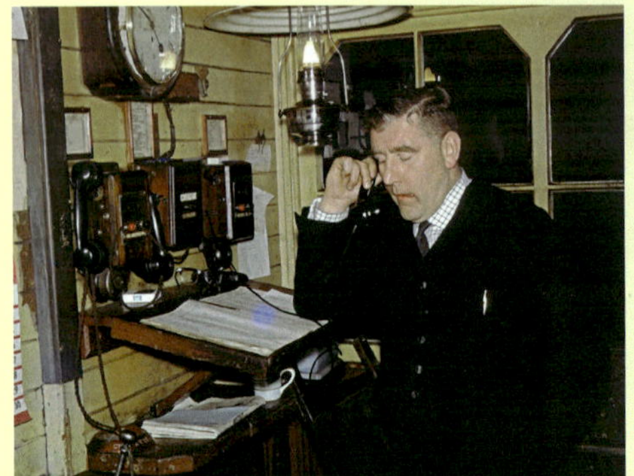

RIBBLEHEAD Bill Sharpe was the last station master and weather observer at Ribblehead, from 1960 to 1967; the station was then made an unstaffed halt so Bill lost his job. He turned down an offer to be an assistant station manager at Appleby and reverted to signalman, becoming a relief at all cabins on the line from Horton to Ais Gill, so he was able to stay in the station master's house at Ribblehead. He was on duty in Ais Gill cabin at the summit of the line when the 'Farewell to Steam' excursion train passed on its way back to Liverpool on 11 August 1968.

Bill was born in Leeds and lived in the dales country from the age of 14, when he started work on a farm at Ingleton. At 19 he went to work in the granite quarry at Ingleton, then the limestone quarry at Ribblehead. He joined the railway at 27 and stayed at Ribblehead station through three grades of work: porter for 12 months, signalman for eight years and station master for seven years. His son Geoffrey was a signalman at Milnthorpe on the LNWR main line in Westmorland. Bill is pictured on the phone to 'control' at Carlisle on relief signal duty on 7 December 1967.

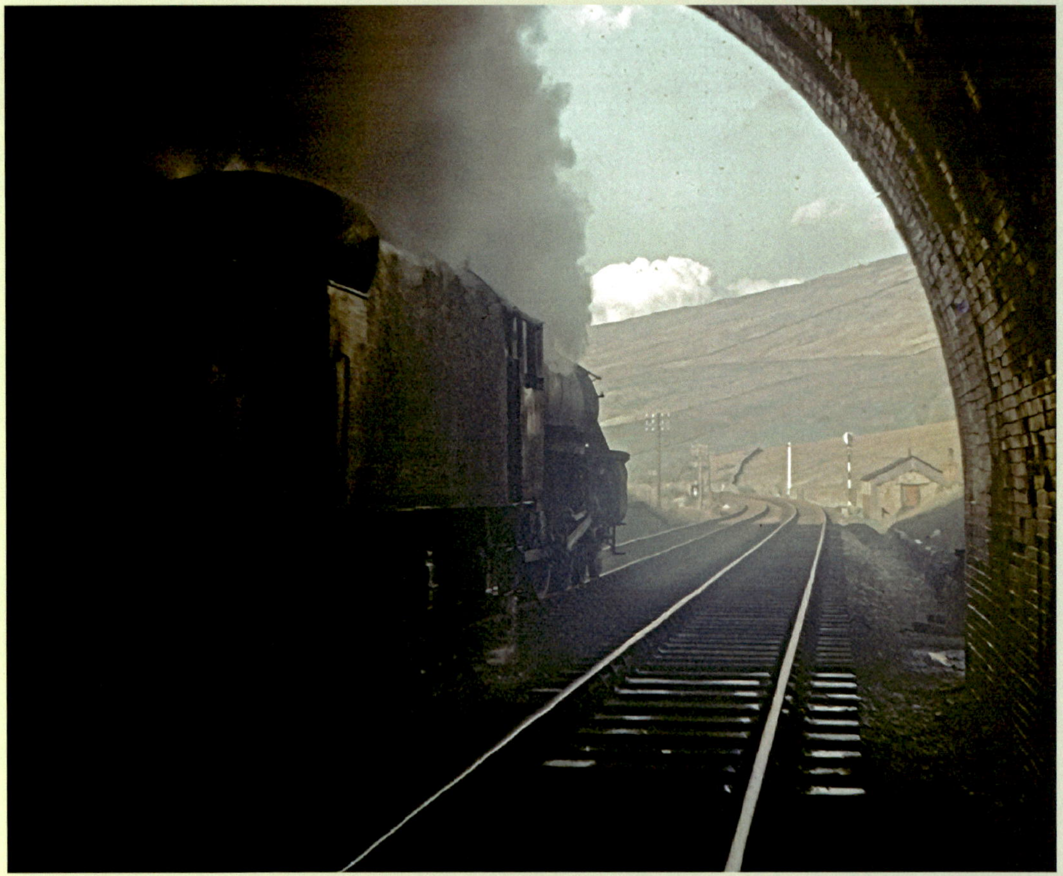

DENT HEAD The 'Long Drag' north of Settle reaches its first summit 1,151 feet above sea level inside Blea Moor Tunnel, 500 feet under the moor. The tunnel is 1½ miles long, dank, smoky and spooky, and conditions were bad for footplate and maintenance men in steam days. Now over the crest and gathering speed on a downhill run, it will be a relief for the engine crew on 'Black Five' No 45131 (Armstrong Whitworth, 1935) with a northbound freight as it emerges from the north portal of the tunnel into the sunshine and verdant beauty of Dentdale on 12 October 1967.

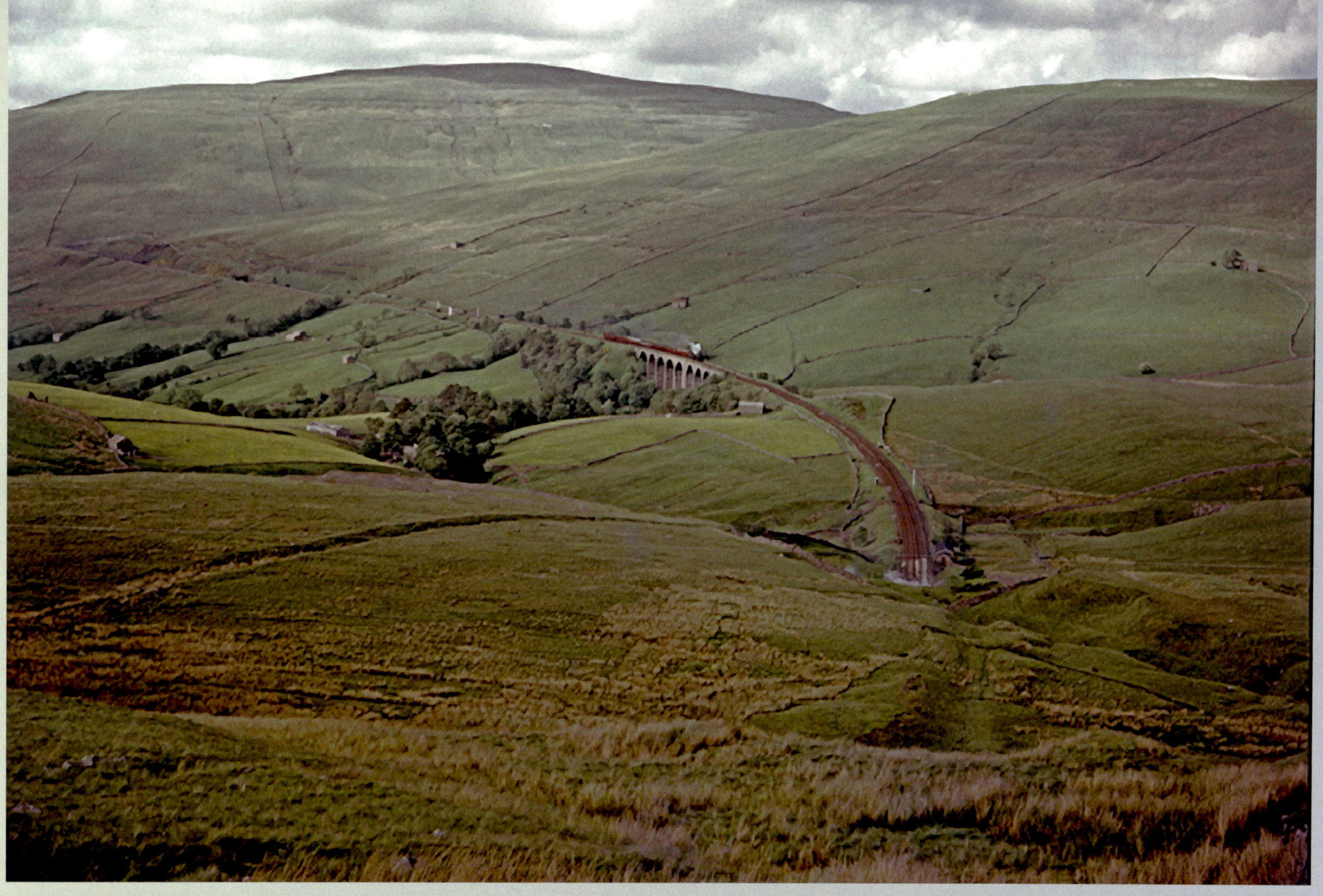

DENTDALE The former Midland Railway Settle-Carlisle main line over the 'roof of England' is viewed from Blea Moor on 19 June 1965. The wisp of steam marks a southbound passenger train crossing Dent Head Viaduct, and we can see steam from a previous train pothering out of the north portal of Blea Moor Tunnel below our location. In December 1963 the line was blocked by snow for a week, mainly by a 60-foot drift over the north portal of this tunnel. The railway cuts a ledge along the side of Widdale Fell (right, 2,203 feet), and Baugh Fell (2,216 feet) rises in the background.

DENT In the late-afternoon sunlight on 20 September 1963, an ex-LMSR 'Jubilee' Class 7P locomotive, with a van and four coaches, stops in Dent station at 5.54pm on a Bradford-Carlisle service. Dent signal cabin and Dent Head Viaduct can be seen in the background with Blea Moor on the right. This station, at 1,145 feet, is 5 miles from and 700 feet higher than the village of the same name. The access road from the valley bottom, first metalled in 1954, climbs 450 feet in three-quarters of a mile, starting with hairpin corners on a 1 in 5 gradient. Dent station is still open as a halt and the building on the right is now a guest house.

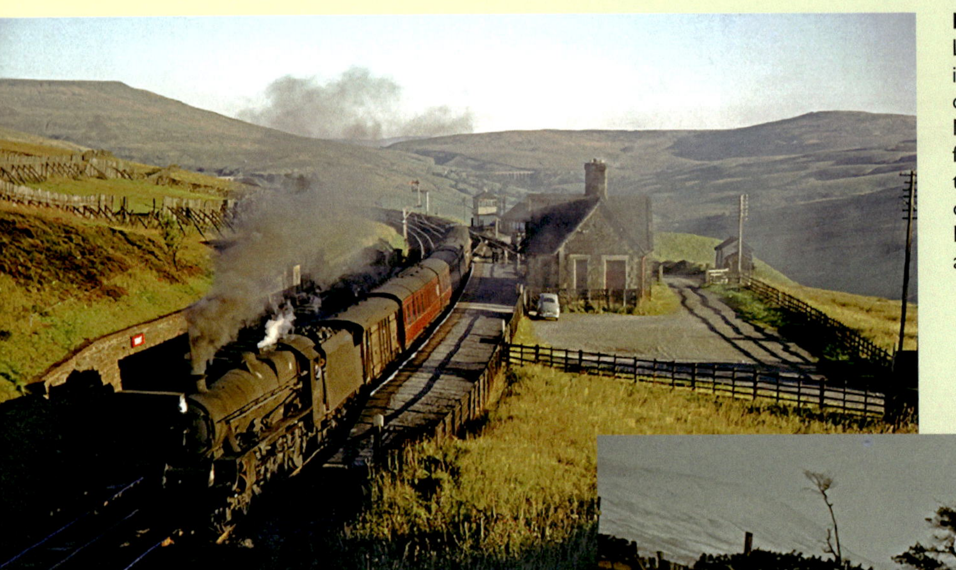

DENT With light snow on the ground and its steam backlit by the sun, a 'Black Five', fitted with a small snowplough, brings a Bradford to Carlisle stopping train into Dent station, the highest in England, on 19 January 1966.

DENT The streamlined 1959 Morris Minor car parked here looks out of place in the quaint main street, named simply The Street, on the road through Dentdale on 1 June 1961. The street is roughly paved with cobbles (not granite setts) the full width of the street between the buildings with no footpaths. On the right is a drinking fountain, roughly hewn from red Shap granite, in memory of Adam Sedgwick (1785-1873) of Dent, one of the founders of the science of geology. The Sun Inn stands at the top of the street where it zigzags out of the village towards Sedbergh, the nearest town, 5½ miles north-west.

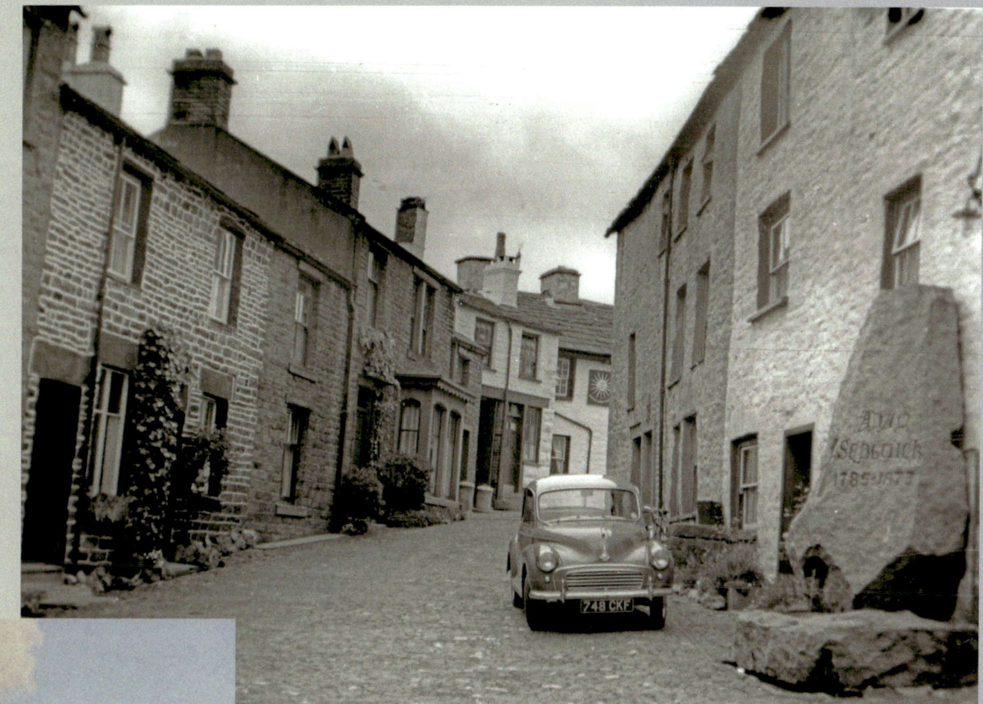

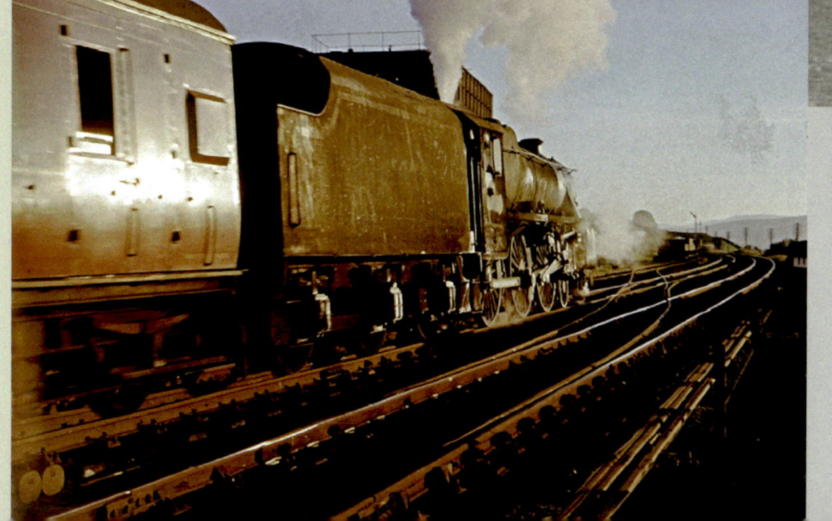

GARSDALE With the evening sunlight glinting on its siderods, 'Black Five' No 44900, built at Crewe in 1945, pulls out of Garsdale station at 6.30pm with a Carlisle to Bradford stopping train on 20 September 1963. On the other side of the engine can be seen the water tank, which stood on a stone building housing the Tank House Meeting Room, the social centre of the district with a stage, a piano and upholstered seats. As the railway had to follow the contours of the land, Garsdale station is at the head of the dale, 3 miles from the hamlet and church of the same name, but it was originally named Hawes Junction; a Midland branch ran from here to Hawes, where it met the NER Wensleydale branch from Northallerton. The junction and branch closed in 1959.

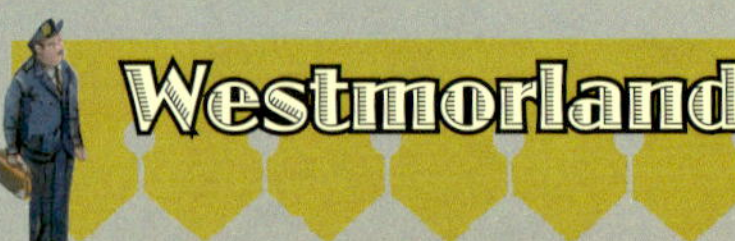

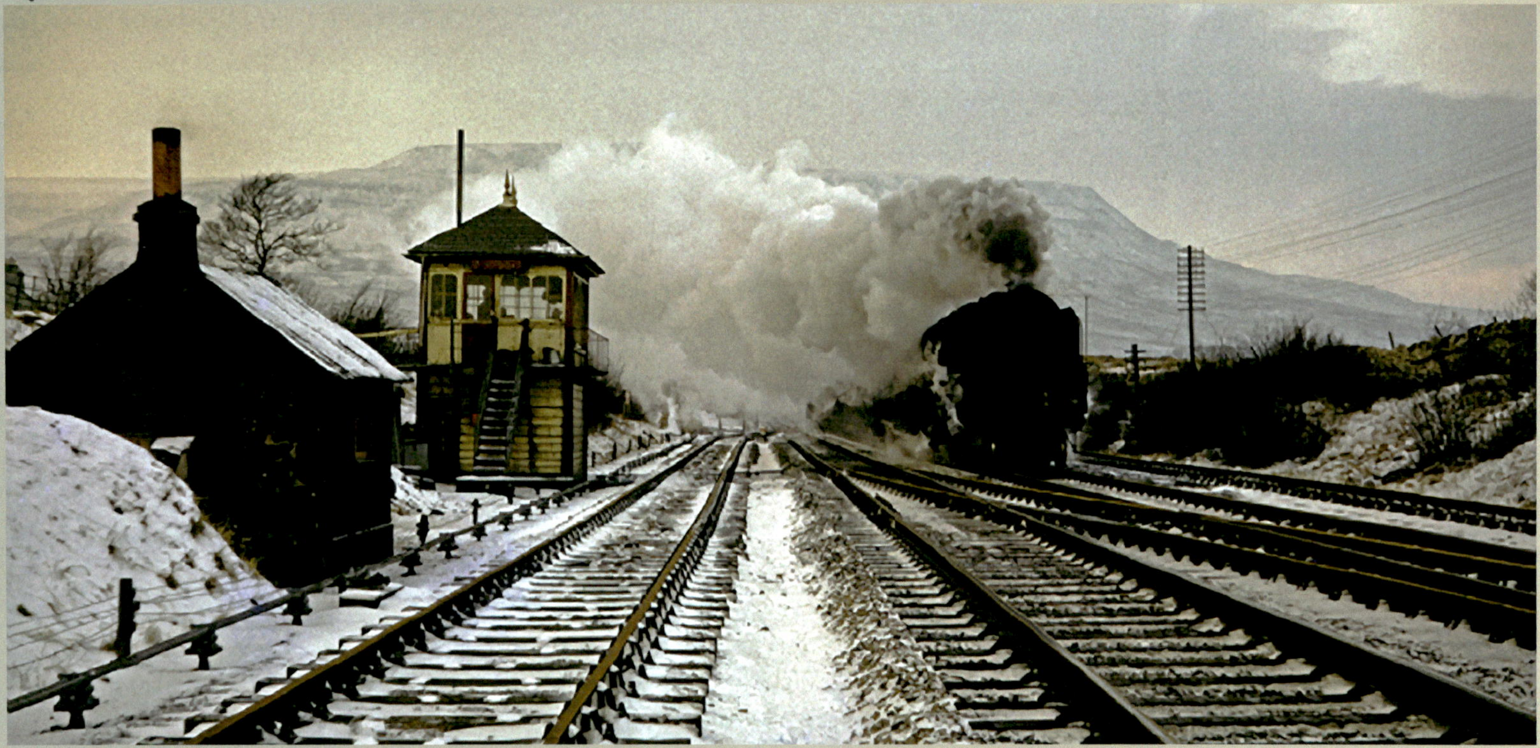

AIS GILL The former Midland Railway main line to the north reaches the 1,169-foot summit on the watershed and county boundary with this view north from Yorkshire into Westmorland. Here a big BR Standard 9F 2-10-0 locomotive crests the summit with a heavy load of anhydrite southbound from Long Meg Quarry in Cumberland to Widnes on 19 January 1966. It was the coldest day since the notorious winter of 1947, with a maximum temperature of 28 degrees F (-2½ degrees C), and the smoke and steam shows up boldly in the cold air. The four-track layout here provided loop sidings for slow, loose-coupled goods trains to stand by for fast, continuous air-braked freight and passenger trains to pass. The standard MR signal cabin was built in 1900 and is now preserved at the Midland Railway Centre, Butterley, Derbyshire. The stone bothy is a platelayers' hut. In the background is Wild Boar Fell (2,324 feet), below which the railway curves right over Ais Gill Beck and past Aisgill hamlet, the nearest habitation, as it descends into Mallerstang.

Right: **MALLERSTANG** 'Long Meg' on the 'Long Drag': another hulking, grimy 9F plods slowly up Mallerstang with the heavy, metallic clank-clank of its coupling rods as it toils up final stretch of the steady 1 in 100 gradient for 16 miles on the northern ascent to Ais Gill summit on 9 June 1967. This train, like the one we saw opposite, was known as 'Long Meg', a twice-daily load of anhydrite from Long Meg Quarry to Widnes chemical works and the heaviest train on the 'Long Drag'. In latter years it was always hauled by a 9F, this one being No 92208. As it approached this location the exhaust echoed against the escarpment of Wild Boar Fell high above the line on the west side, and on a still day the laboured beat of the steam exhaust could be heard for 2 minutes into the distance towards the summit. Mallerstang is a wide, U-shaped, glaciated valley cradling the headwaters of the River Eden, which flows by Appleby and Carlisle into the Solway Firth.

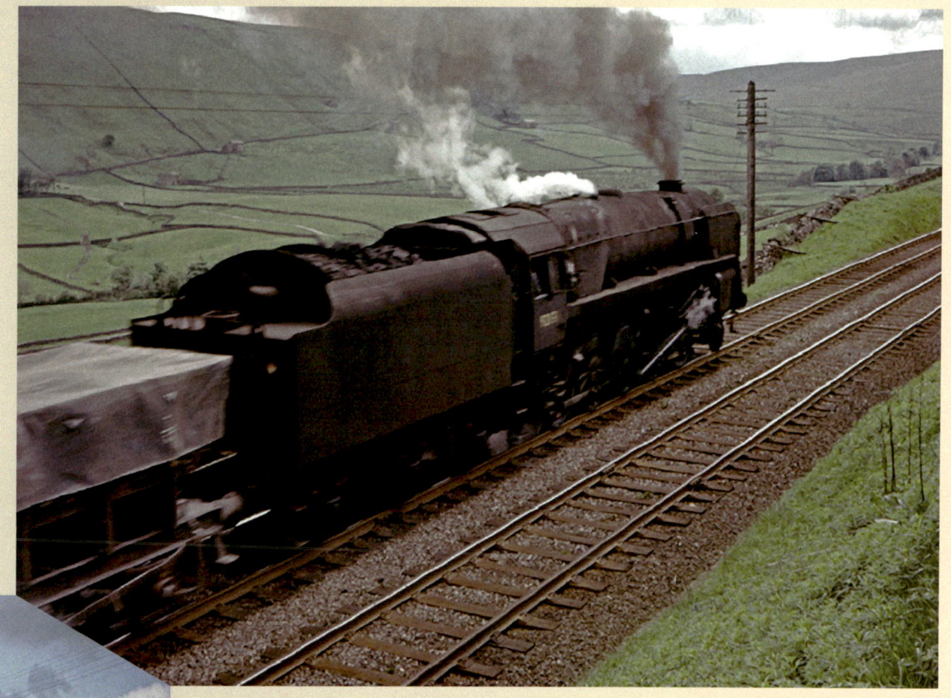

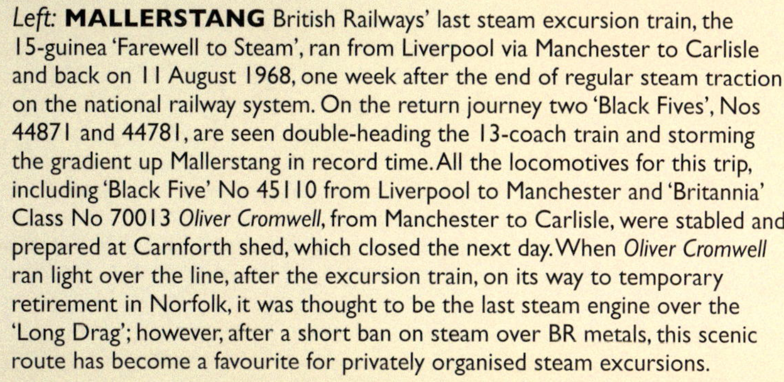

Left: **MALLERSTANG** British Railways' last steam excursion train, the 15-guinea 'Farewell to Steam', ran from Liverpool via Manchester to Carlisle and back on 11 August 1968, one week after the end of regular steam traction on the national railway system. On the return journey two 'Black Fives', Nos 44871 and 44781, are seen double-heading the 13-coach train and storming the gradient up Mallerstang in record time. All the locomotives for this trip, including 'Black Five' No 45110 from Liverpool to Manchester and 'Britannia' Class No 70013 *Oliver Cromwell*, from Manchester to Carlisle, were stabled and prepared at Carnforth shed, which closed the next day. When *Oliver Cromwell* ran light over the line, after the excursion train, on its way to temporary retirement in Norfolk, it was thought to be the last steam engine over the 'Long Drag'; however, after a short ban on steam over BR metals, this scenic route has become a favourite for privately organised steam excursions.

DALLAM railway viaduct over the River Bela and its water meadows was a dramatic feature of the landscape between Milnthorpe and Sandside. This 300-yard viaduct on 23 stone arches and three steel arches carried the 5-mile single-line branch of the Furness Railway from Arnside to Hincaster, where it linked with the LNWR main line. Intermediate stations were at Sandside and Heversham. The link was built mainly to carry coke trains from County Durham that went via Tebay to the iron and steel works in Furness. It was also used by stopping passenger trains from Grange-over-Sands to Kendal, excursion trains from Leeds to Windermere via Carnforth, and a fortnightly special train carrying Durham miners to a convalescent home at Conishead near Ulverston. Passenger services on the branch ended in 1942 but coke trains and excursions continued to use it till it closed on 9 September 1963, one month before this photograph was taken, following the demise of the Furness iron industry. The viaduct was demolished in 1966 but the line from Arnside to Sandside quarry remained open for stone trains till 1971. Here the River Bela flows into the River Kent estuary, seen beyond the viaduct, with Whitbarrow (706 feet) in the background.

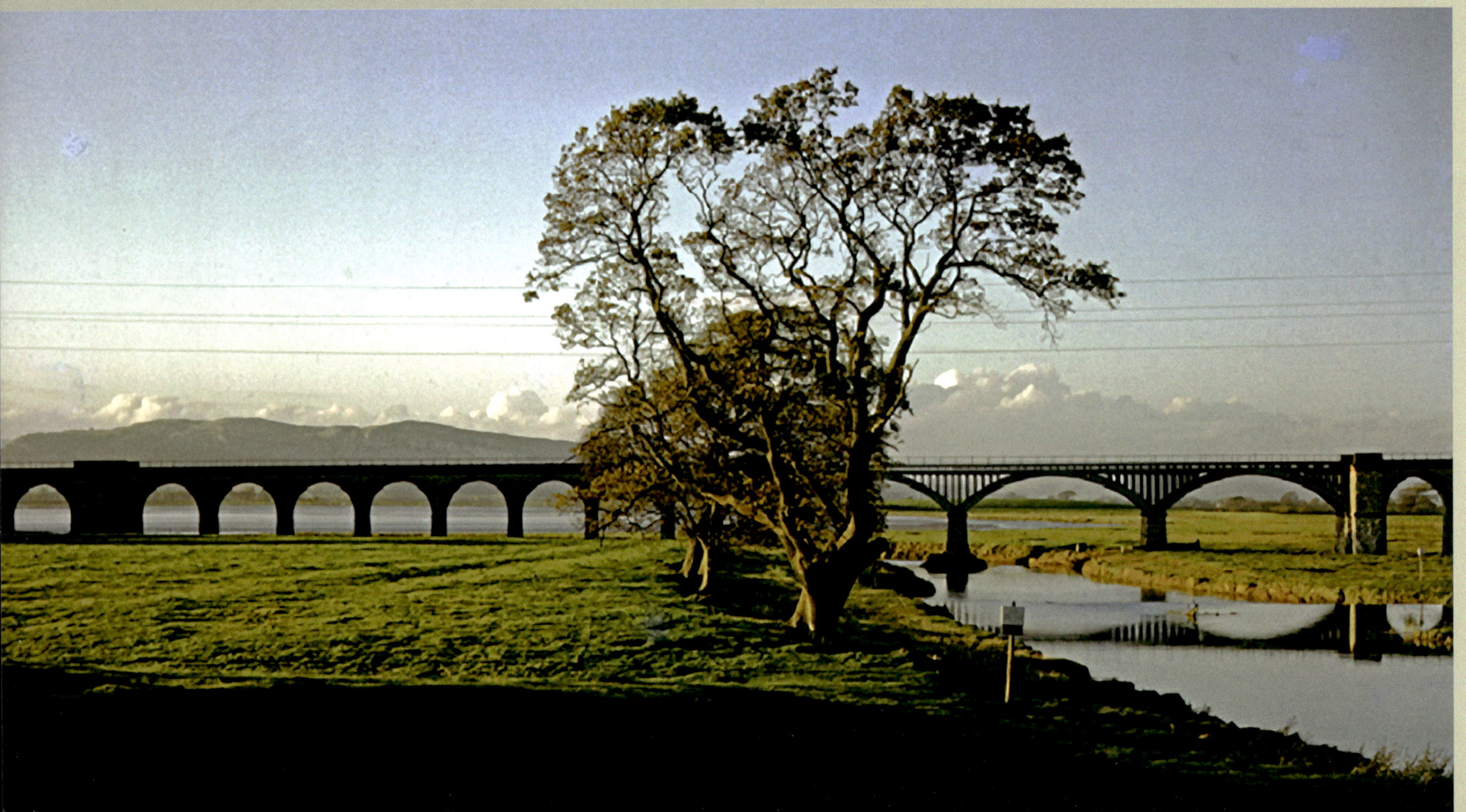

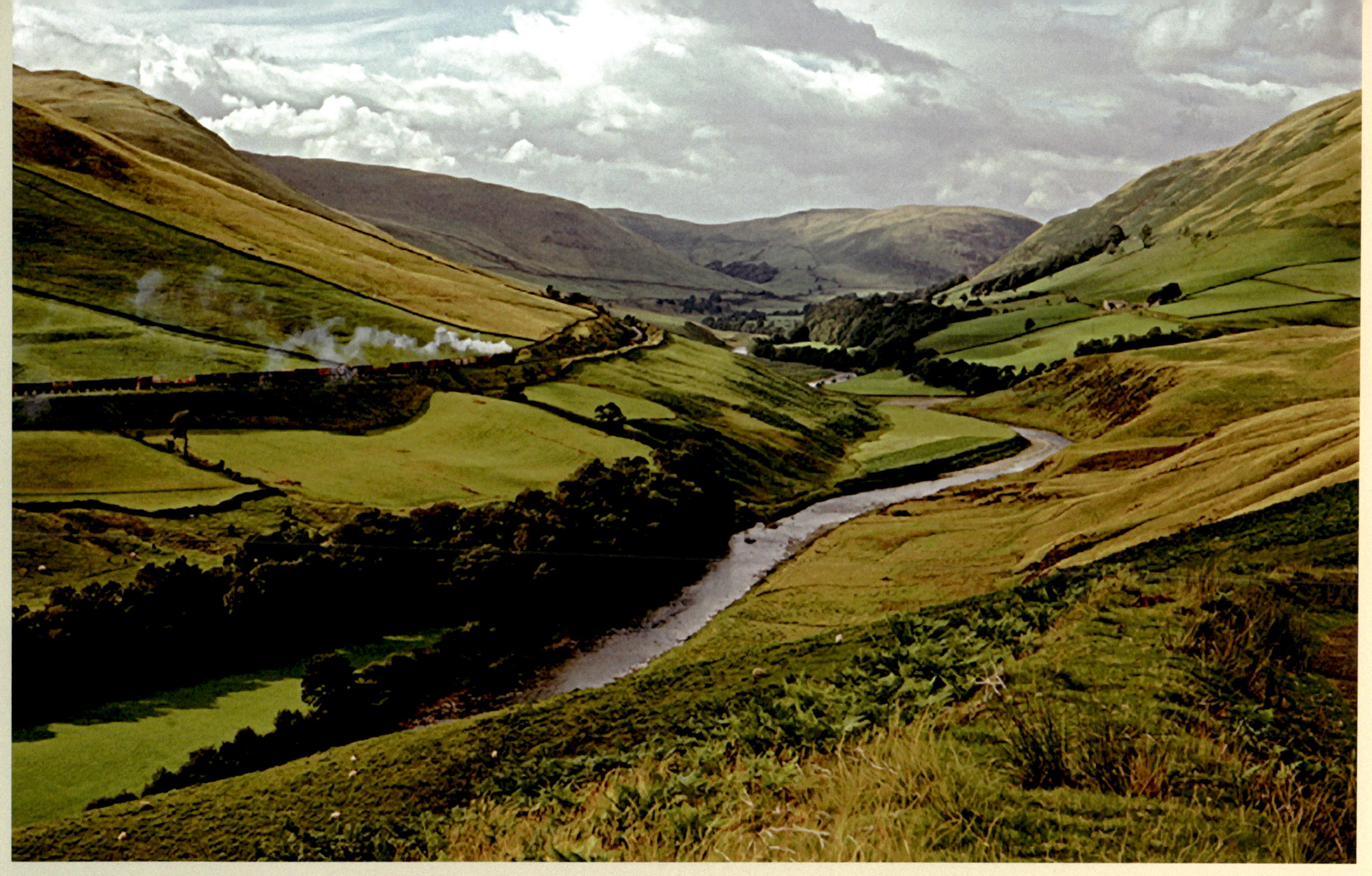

LONSDALE The trail of steam along the far fellside is from a northbound goods train on the former LNWR West Coast Main Line hugging the slopes of Dillicar Common between Grayrigg and Tebay on 15 August 1963. The line swung east from Kentdale to Lonsdale to take advantage of the gap cut by the River Lune through the fells linking the North Pennine Moors to the east with the Cumbrian Mountains to the west, giving trains an easier assault on the climb to 916 feet over Shap Fells. The Lune rises in Ravenstonedale and flows south by Kirkby Lonsdale and Lancaster to the sea. Dieselisation of BR saw the last ordinary steam passenger and freight trains pass through these fells in December 1967. The M6 motorway opened in 1970 with a two-tier ledge along the fellside above the railway, then in 1974 the railway was electrified with overhead gantries and catenary.

GRAYRIGG
Cresting Grayrigg bank on the climb from Oxenholme, 'Black Five' No 45481 heads a northbound freight through the site of the former Grayrigg station on the West Coast Main Line between Lancaster and Carlisle on 1 May 1963, with Grayrigg signal cabin in the rear.

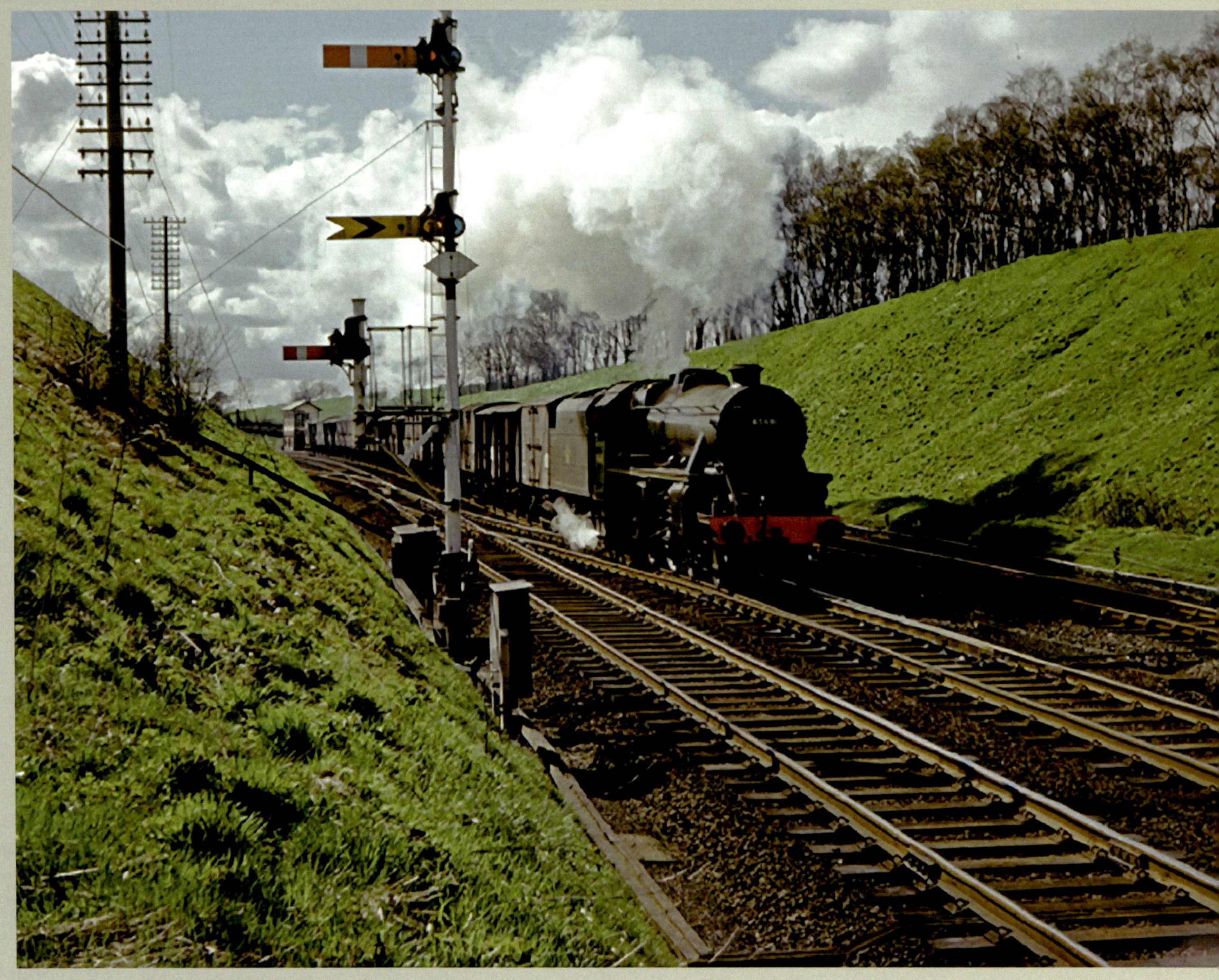

OXENHOLME

station on the former LNWR main line, seen here on 29 May 1962, was the junction for the branch to Kendal and Windermere. The covered bay platform and sidings on the left were for branch traffic. From here northbound trains on the main line begin the ascent of Grayrigg bank, the first part of the climb to Shap summit, and steam freight and passenger trains could whistle up a banking engine from the sidings behind the camera if they needed a push up the side of Hay Fell. Oxenholme, with its engine shed, freight yard, signal cabin and station offices, was a railwaymen's village, but it was in decline at this time together with the railways. The engine shed closed in 1962 and the goods and banking engine sidings were lifted in 1969.

In 1973 the main line was electrified as part of the West Coast route to Scotland, the Windermere branch was singled, the signal cabins closed and the semaphore signals were replaced with colour lights. The sidings on the left have been replaced by a car park and the island platform buildings have been demolished, but the overall canopy remains and the station looks much the same today, although it has been fancifully renamed Oxenholme (The Lake District), even though it is not in the Lake District; the National Park boundary is 5½ miles down the Windermere branch.

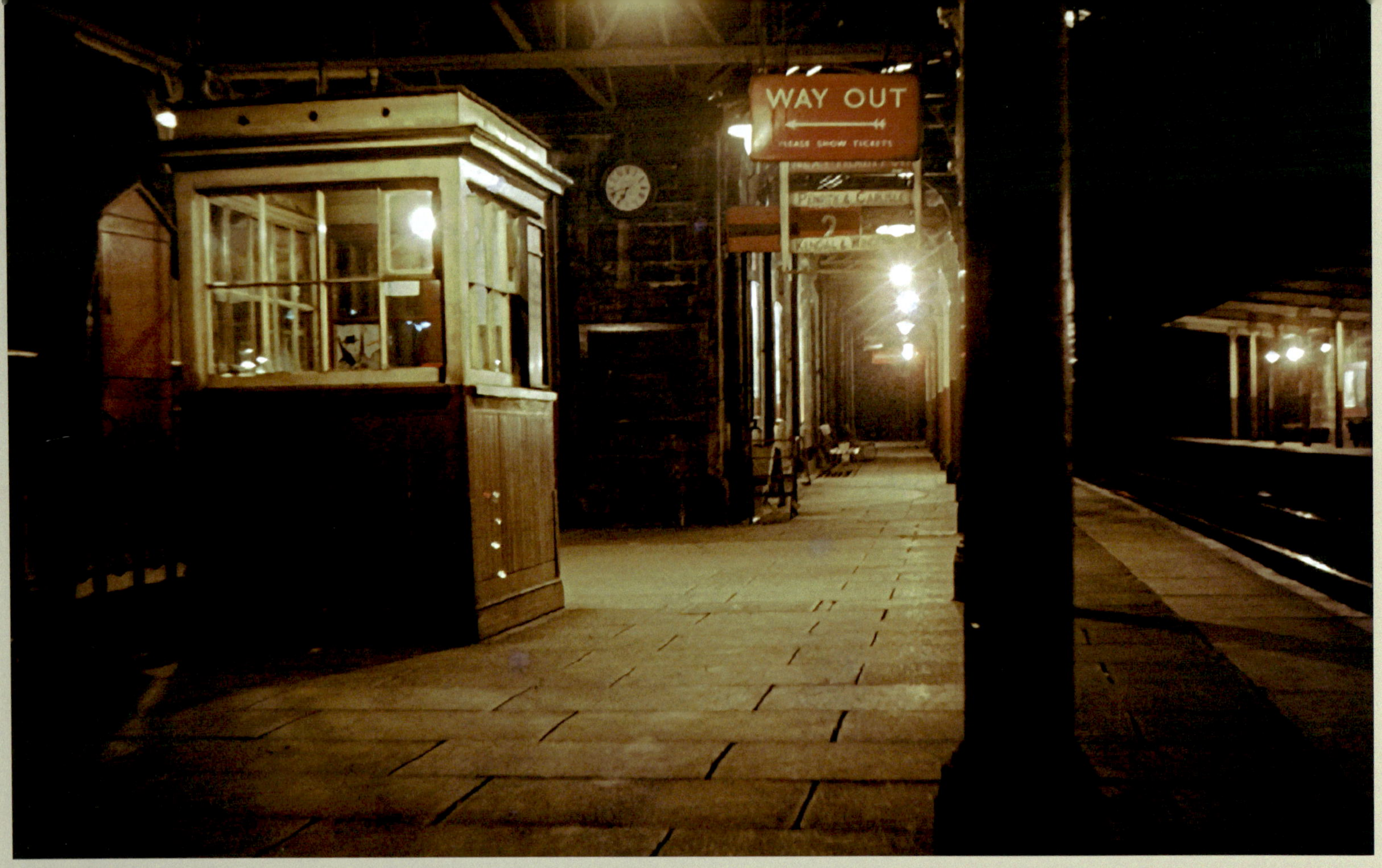

OXENHOLME station by gaslight, looking north along the down main platform on 16 February 1968. The picture shows the porter/ticket collector's cabin, the destination boards, the clock and the stonework of the station buildings. This station was the scene of a murder at 3.15am on 10 February 1965 when three policemen were shot – one fatally, one seriously injured – when they cornered a gunman in the waiting room on the up main platform (right). The man was wanted for using a gun when police searching for a burglar stopped a stolen van. There followed an armed manhunt over the fells south-east of the station at daylight when four farmers chased a man one of them spotted running across the fields, and joined in the hunt with their shotguns as police from three counties converged on the area with 30 rifles and 100 revolvers. After a 1½-mile chase over The Helm ridge and across fields, a shot in the leg from a farmer and a grazed temple from a police shot brought him down near Blease Farm and he was arrested.

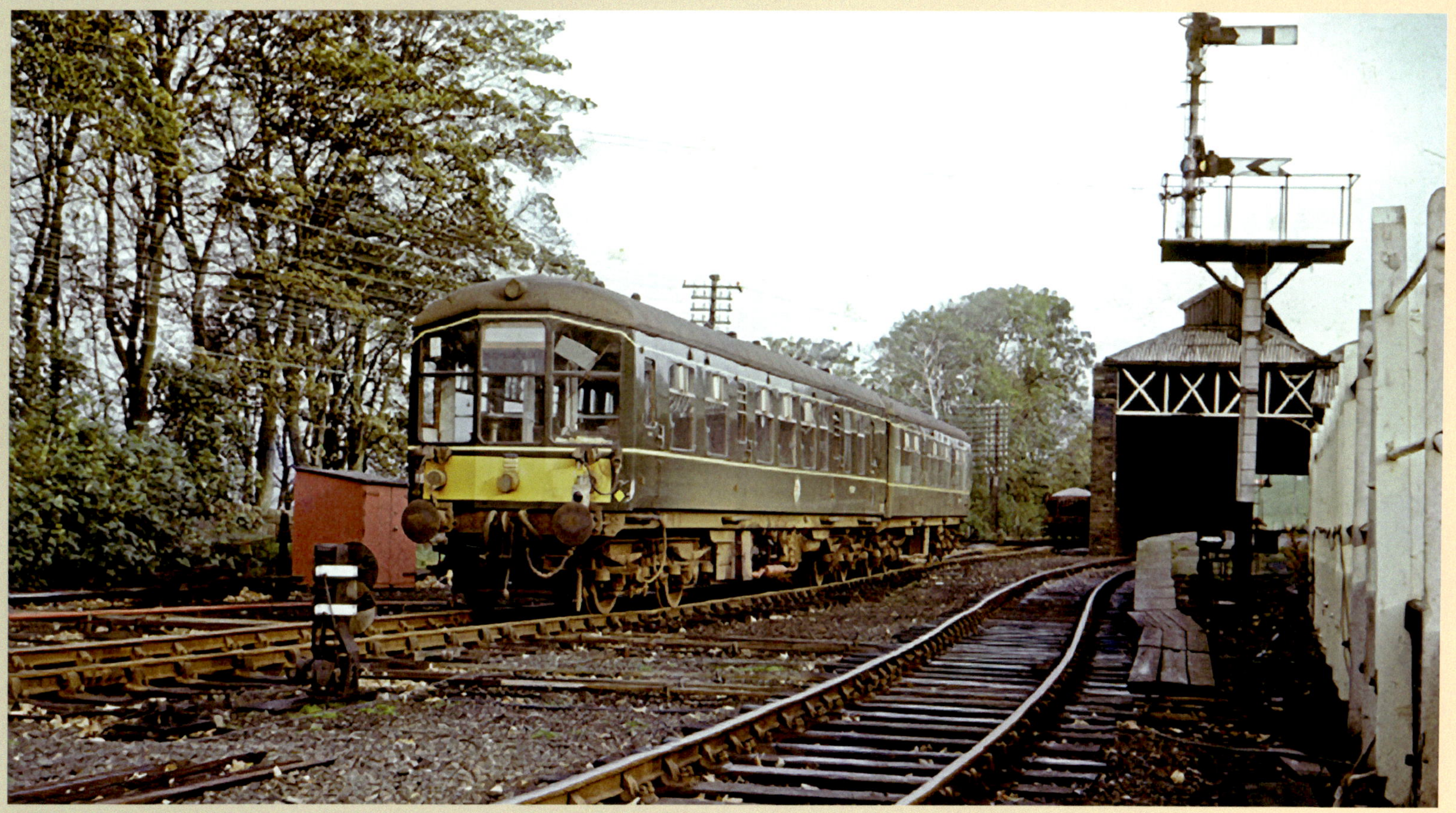

OXENHOLME This two-car diesel multiple unit, seen on a siding at Oxenholme station, was one of the second batch of BR Derby lightweight units with AEC engines built in 1954-55 for services between Carlisle, Penrith and Whitehaven. This set worked on the Carlisle-Silloth branch from 1954 till the line closed in 1964. These sets later saw service between Carlisle and Skipton and on 18 April 1966 they inaugurated a diesel service on the Windermere branch, operating between Windermere and Carnforth. They were ideal for passengers viewing the scenery through the large, observation-style windscreens with glazing between the passenger saloons and the motorman's cab instead of the opaque partitions on later DMUs. The yellow warning panel replaced the original cream 'moustache' on the dash panels of these early DMUs. Hundreds more steam trains ran on the Windermere branch in the next two years because of frequent breakdowns of diesel locomotives and multiple units, and these ex-west Cumberland DMUs were scrapped in 1967-68.

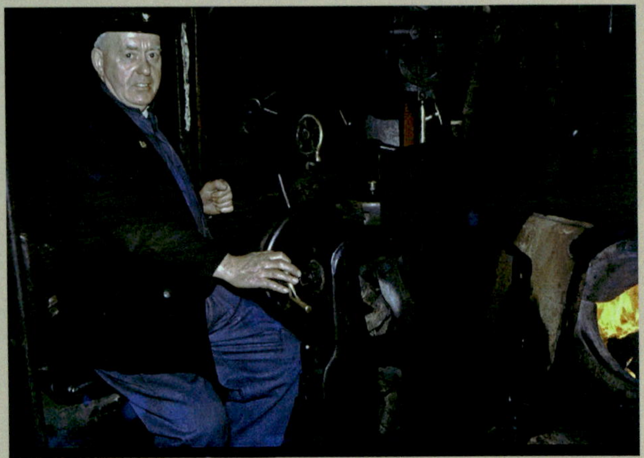

KENDAL Driver Joe Wilson of Carnforth shed is in the cab of BR Standard 9F No 92009 shunting Kendal goods yard on 15 February 1968.

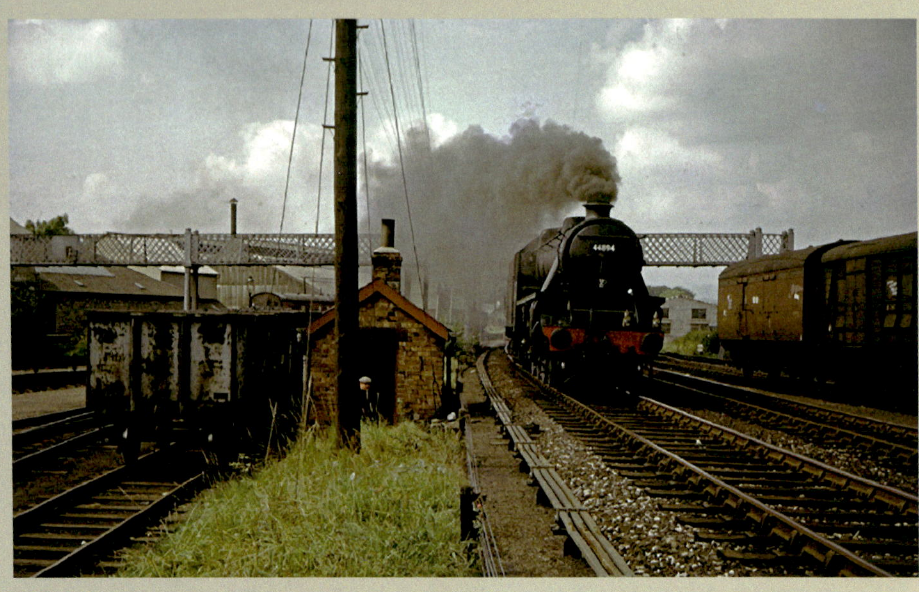

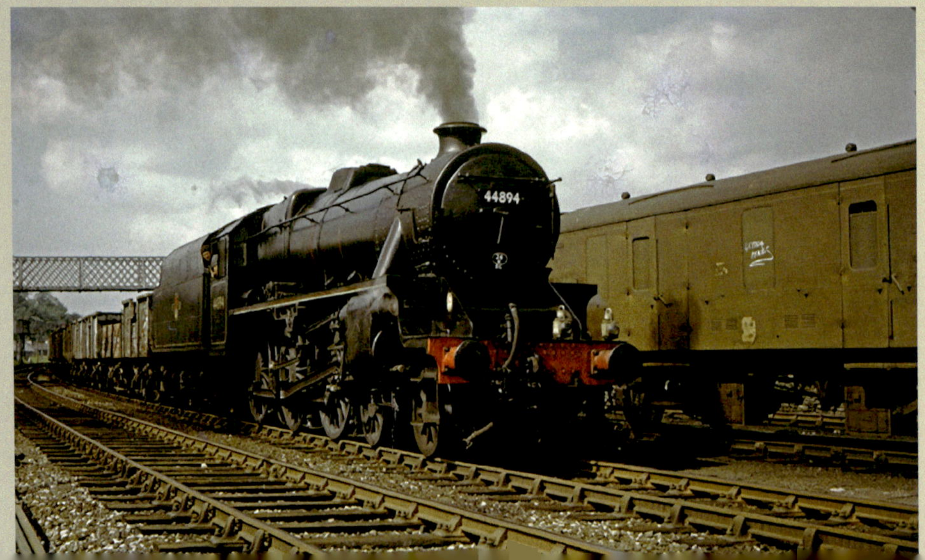

KENDAL After shunting the goods yard (left), 'Black Five' No 44894 (Crewe, 1945) is running around its train (which is just out of sight) on the running lines at Kendal before taking it away to Carnforth at 2.25pm on 1 August 1968, two days before the end of steam on BR. Most steam engines were neglected and filthy in the last months of steam traction, so No 44894 had been cleaned by a band of railfans for photography. The parcels van sidings are on the right; the vans will be loaded with parcels and mailbags in Kendal station platform later in the day.

KENDAL The crimson Ribble buses add colour to the main street of the 'Auld Grey Town' (their paintwork has been rendered lighter by Kodachrome film). In this picture on 5 March 1962 a 1950 low-bridge double-decker is at the stop by the Town Hall on Highgate on the 55-mile route 68 from Keswick to Lancaster. This is an all-Leyland bus as both the chassis and the body are by Leyland Motors; it is also advertising Leyland Paints, made in the same town in south Lancashire. Low-bridge buses were used on this route to negotiate the railway bridge at Carnforth. The Ribble single-decker passing the Town Hall is a 1951 Weymann-bodied Leyland Olympic on a town service.

Today this is a one-way street, with northbound traffic turning right or left at the signals by the Town Hall, and the street over the brow is a pedestrian zone with limited access for motor vehicles. The Town Hall was built piecemeal from 1825 to 1897 and the clock tower of 1861 strikes the hours and the quarters and a carillon plays a different folk tune for each day of the week every three hours from 9.00am to 6.00pm. The Town Hall was home to Kendal Municipal Borough Council till 1974, when five local councils were amalgamated to form South Lakeland District Council, now based here.

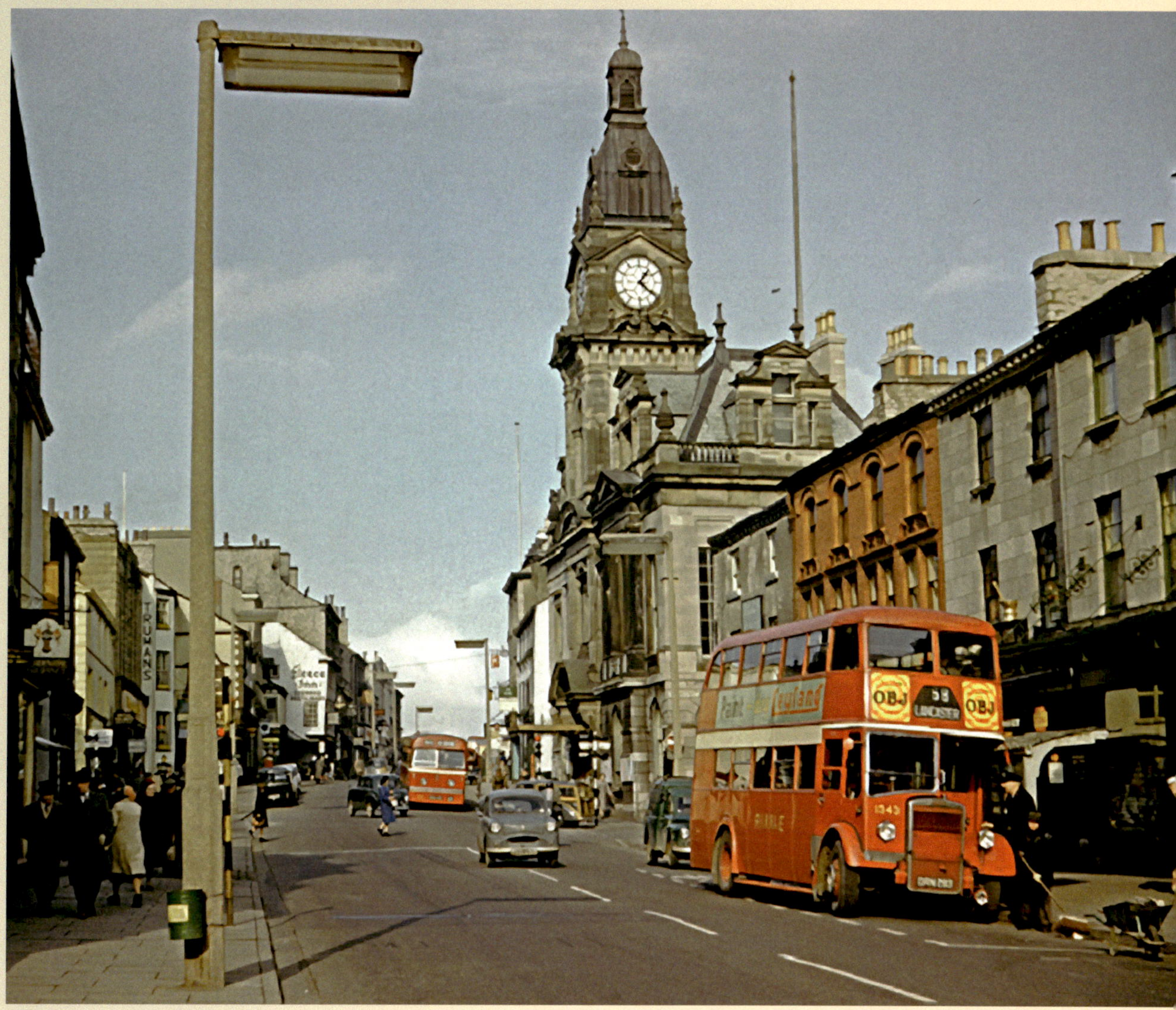

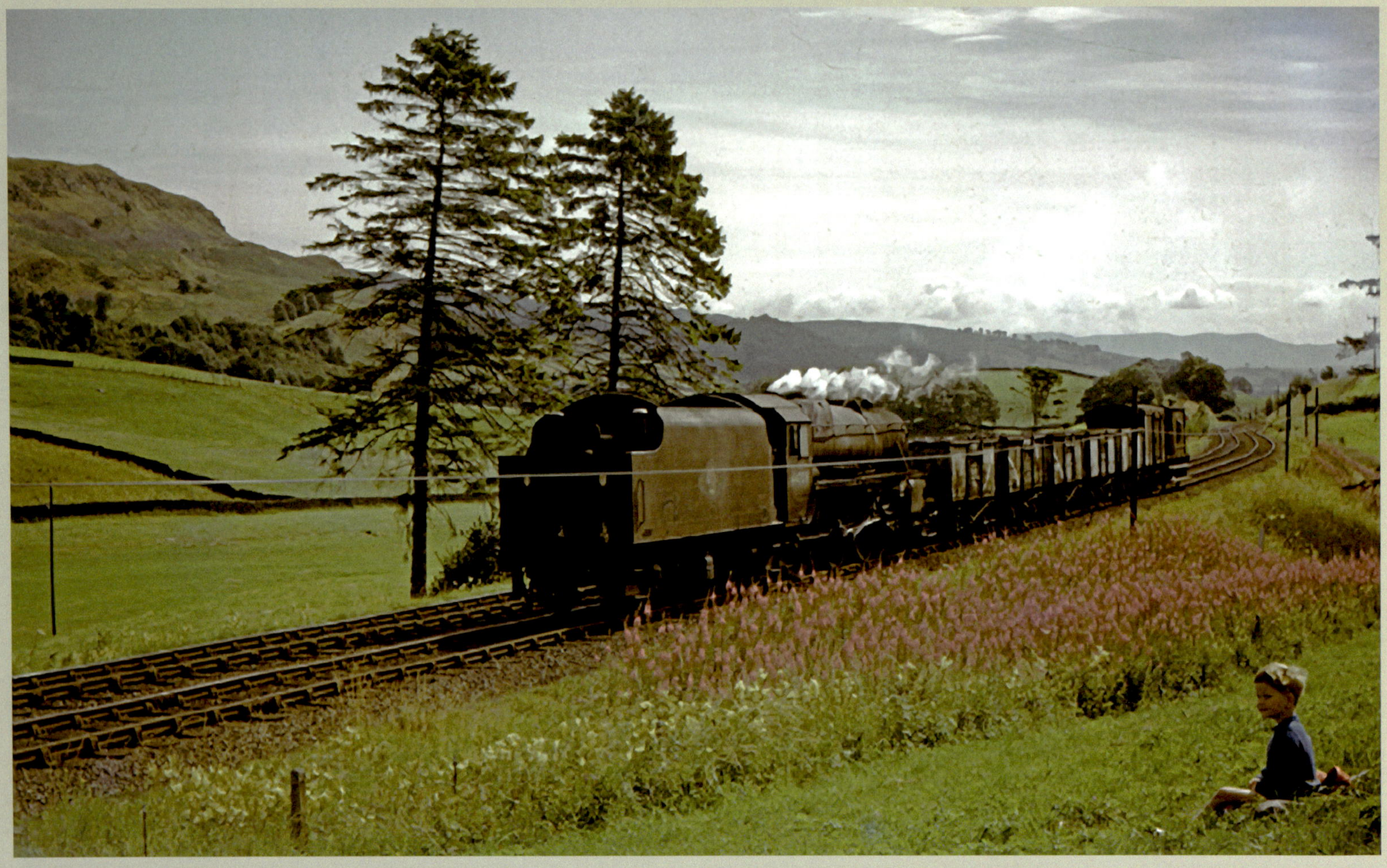

STAVELEY The last steam freight to Windermere, headed by 'Black Five' No 44709 (Horwich, 1948) runs tender-first west of Staveley on 2 August 1968, two days before the end of regular steam workings on British Railways. This was the last steam engine to shunt Kendal goods yard, on Saturday 3 August, and as there was no freight on Sundays it was the last steam engine on the branch. On the left are the slopes of Hugill Fell; on the right is Karl Greenwood, aged 3.

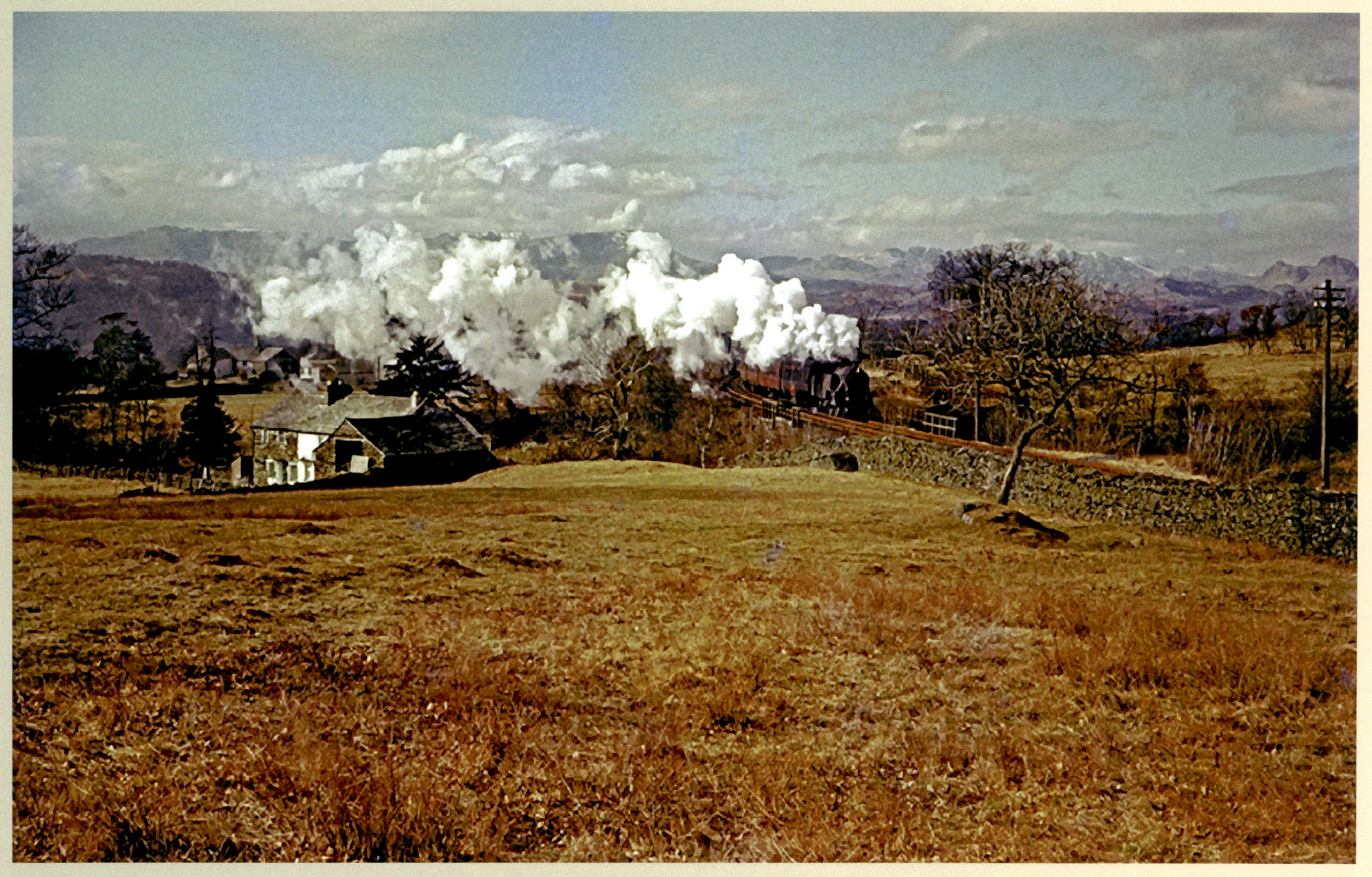

WINDERMERE 'Shovelling white steam over her shoulder', an ex-LMSR 4MT 2-6-4 tank engine lifts a passenger train out of Windermere on its way to Lancaster on 25 February 1965. Steam lingers in the crisp air, almost obscuring the panoramic view of the Cumbrian Mountains with snow on the peaks.

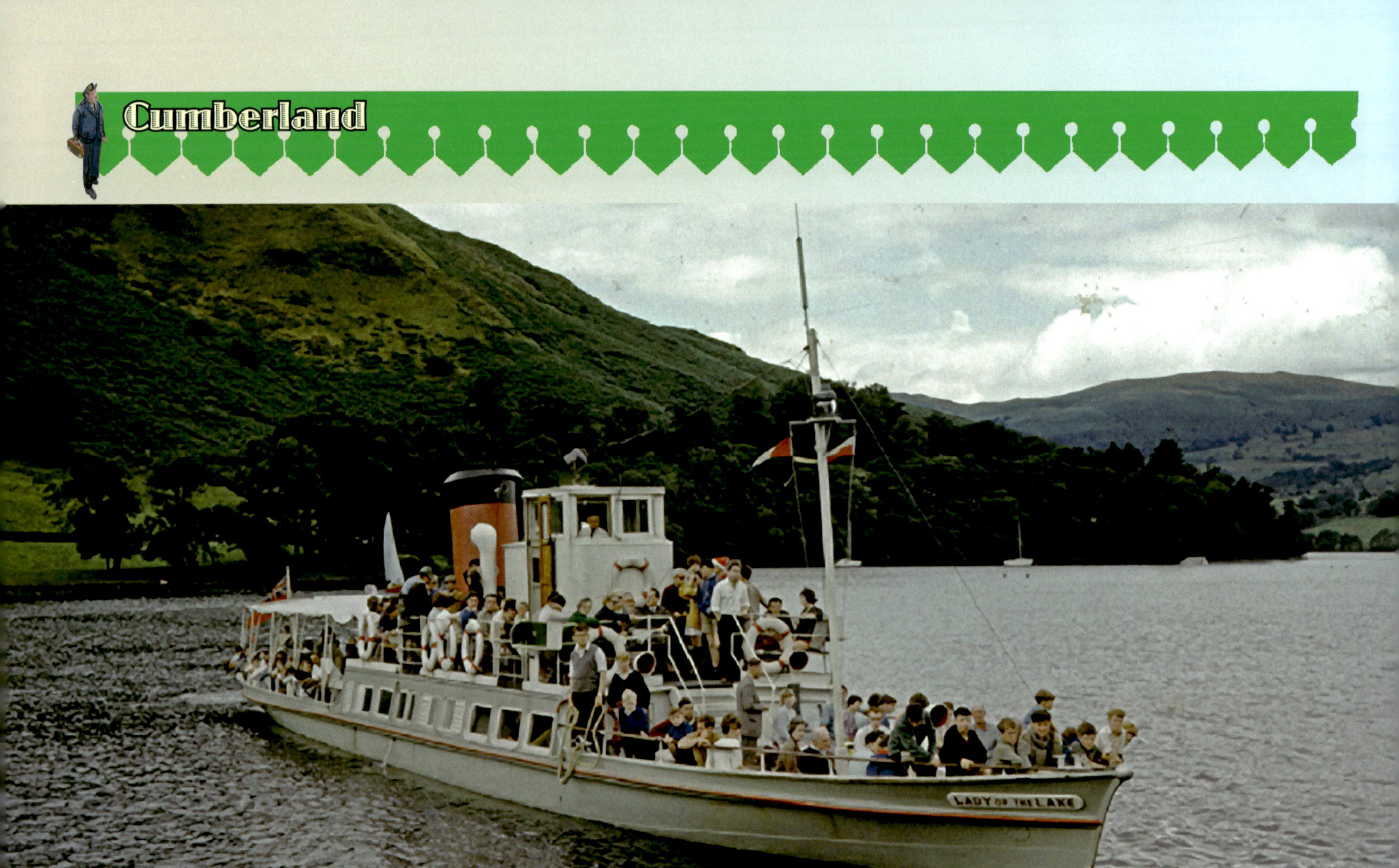

LADY OF THE LAKE

Left: **ULLSWATER** The motor yacht *Lady of the Lake* is one of the oldest vessels afloat, dating from 1877, and is seen arriving at Howtown pier on 1 August 1964. The Ullswater Navigation & Transit Company plies a cruise and ferry service along the length of the lake between Glenridding, Howtown and Pooley Bridge all the year round. The *Lady of the Lake* was built by T. B. Seath at Rutherglen, Glasgow, as a single-screw steam yacht, 97 feet by 15 feet by 2ft 5in, 45 gross tons and licensed to carry 110 passengers. She was taken in three sections by train to Penrith and by horse waggon to Ullswater for reassembly, and entered service as a Royal Mail steamer carrying mails as well as passengers between the lakeside communities she served. Her sister, the *Raven*, was built by T. B. Seath in 1889. Both vessels were converted from steam to diesel motor yachts in 1935 and are still in service together with more modern vessels, thanks to a change of command in 1954 when Sir Wavell (later Lord) Wakefield of Kendal bought a majority share in the company to save it from closing down. The year after this photograph was taken, the *Lady of the Lake* was badly damaged by fire from a shed blaze while she was on the slipway near Pooley Bridge and she was out of service for 14 years before being restored with a new engine and relaunched in 1979.

Ullswater is on the boundary between Westmorland and Cumberland; Glenridding and Howtown are in Westmorland while Pooley Bridge and the background to this photograph are in Cumberland. Donald Campbell broke the world water speed record on Ullswater in his jet *Bluebird K7* in 1955 with an average speed of 202.32mph over the measured mile. In 1983 a speed limit of 10mph came into force on the lake.

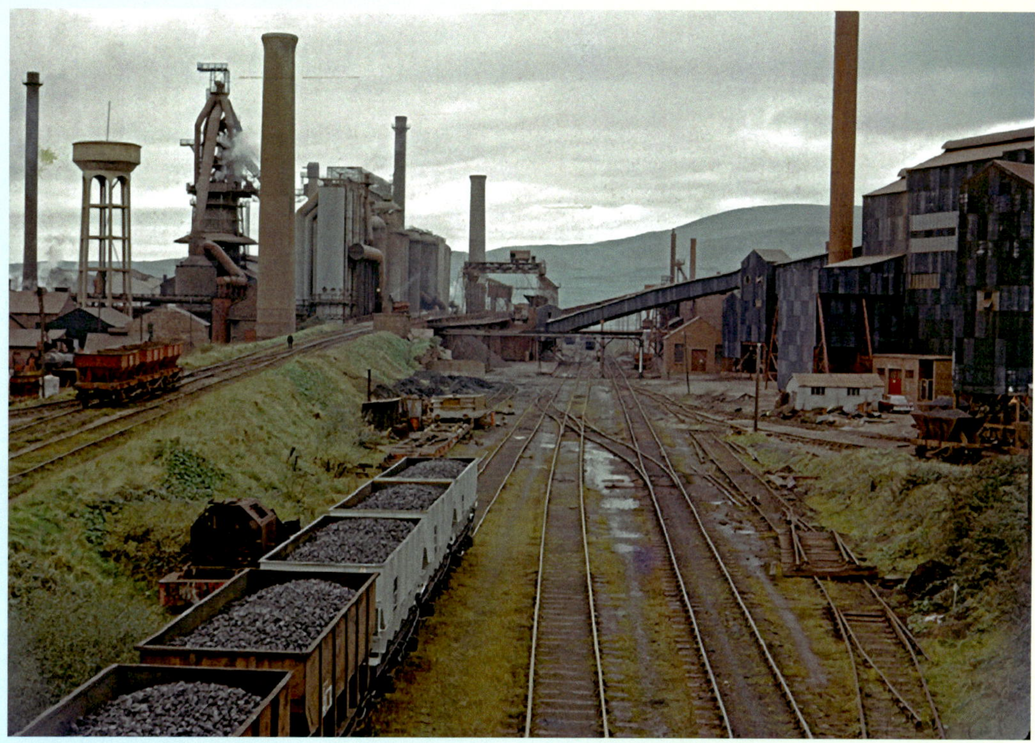

Above: **MILLOM** Ironworks were situated at the southern tip of Cumberland with Black Combe (1,969 feet) in the background. A vast internal railway system served the iron works and the nearby Hodbarrow iron ore mine and connected with the Furness Railway main line between Barrow and Whitehaven. The mine supplied pure haematite iron ore to iron works in Furness for 11 years before the first blast furnace was built here in 1866 between Hodbarrow and the nearby village of Holborn Hill; it subsequently grew into the boom town of Millom (meaning 'at the mills') with terraced houses and public buildings. Hodbarrow mine was on the coast and the mining company built a sea wall in 1900-05 to stop the sea flooding the workings. Eventually the iron ore ran out. This picture of the iron works was taken on 22 October 1967, the year before the mine and works closed down. The two sites have been cleared, except for the slag heaps, and are now wildlife reserves. Millom, the former boom town, is now a depopulated ghost town.

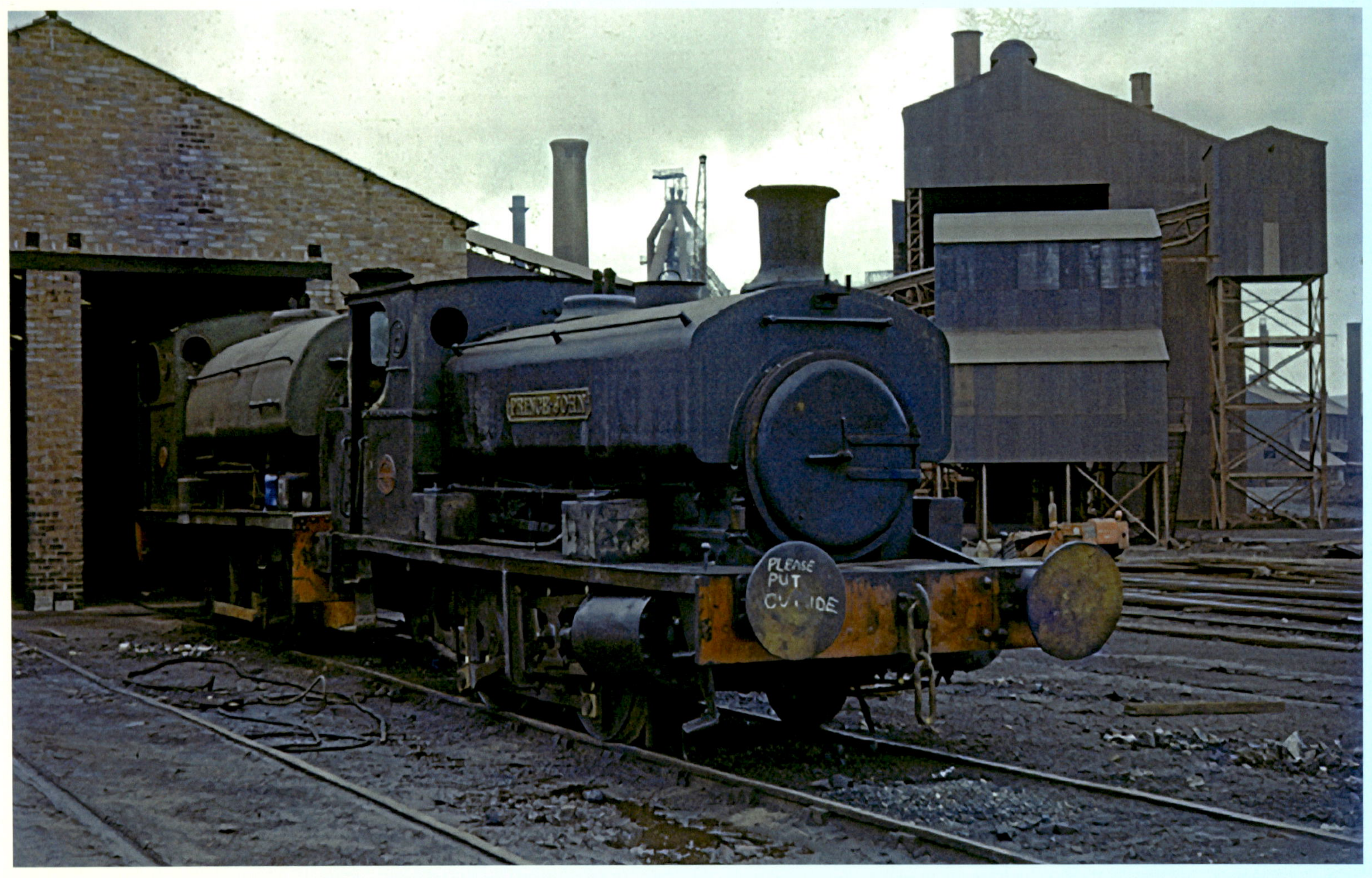

MILLOM Ironworks 0-4-0 saddle-tank engines *Prince John*, built by Andrew Barclay at Kilmarnock in 1918, and No 10, built by Peckett at Bristol in 1934, are pictured outside the engine shed on 22 October 1967.

Right: **DALEGARTH** is the upper terminus of the 7-mile, 1ft 3in-gauge Ravenglass & Eskdale Railway. The locomotive *River Irt*, an 0-8-2, built by the RER in 1928, has turned round on the turntable at the end of the line to run round its train, and the guard is checking and selling tickets for the return run to Ravenglass on 4 June 1961. The railway opened in 1875 as a 3-foot-gauge line terminating a quarter of a mile further up the dale at the village of Boot to carry haematite iron ore from the mines to the Furness Railway main line at Ravenglass. It also carried passengers from 1876 to 1908, but closed in 1913. Then in 1915-17 the model engineer W. J. Basset-Lowke and Narrow Gauge Railways Ltd relaid the track to 1ft 3in gauge from Ravenglass to the present terminus at Dalegarth on a short spur off the original steep route to Boot. This was a passenger railway but it also carried granite from the quarry at Beckfoot to Murthwaite crushing plant from 1922 to 1953. The line was put up for sale in 1960 and saved from closure by the RER Preservation Society with financial backing from Sir Wavell (later Lord) Wakefield of Kendal, saviour of the Ullswater Navigation & Transit Company, and stockbroker Colin Gilbert. Today the railway and the Ullswater company are owned by the Lake District Estates Group controlled by the late Lord Wakefield's descendants.

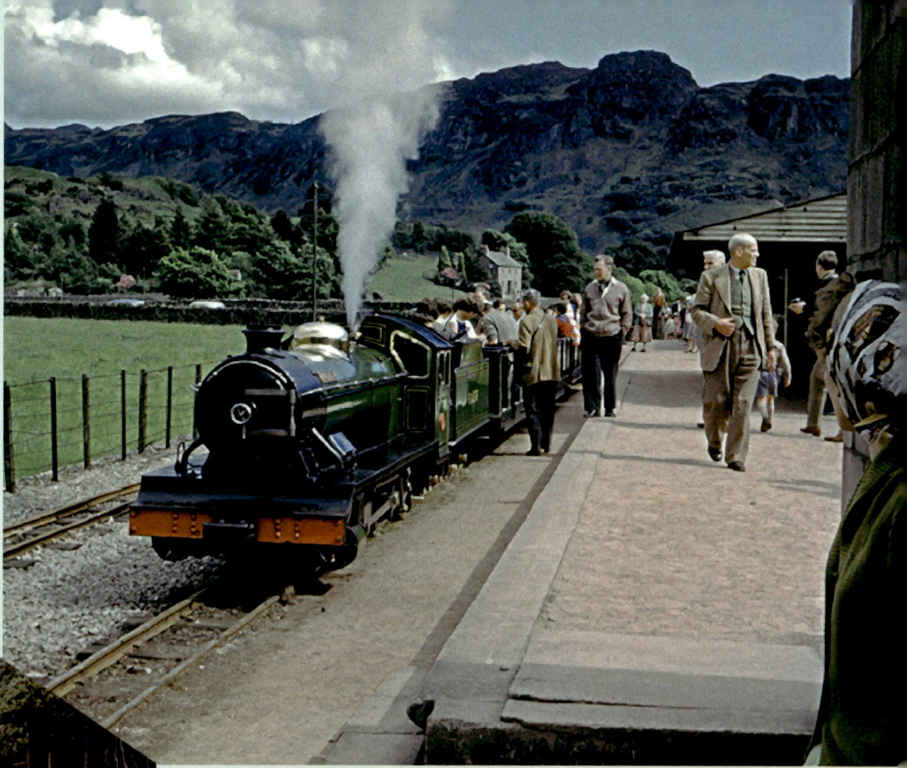

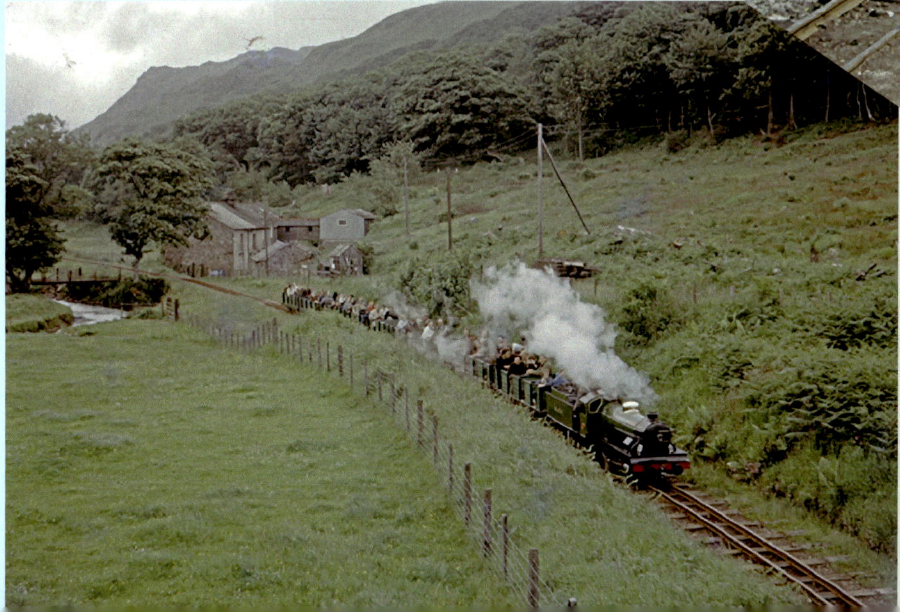

Left: **MUNCASTER** *River Irt* is seen again passing Muncaster Mill with a train on the approach to Ravenglass on 20 June 1965. The watermill, on a race off the River Mite (left), has since been restored to working order. The railway named its three locomotives of that period after the three rivers flowing into the natural harbour at Ravenglass: *River Esk* (a 2-8-2 Davey Paxman of 1923), *River Irt* (see above) and *River Mite* (a 2-8-2 Clarkson of 1967). *River Irt* is now the oldest working 1ft 3in-gauge steam locomotive in the world. Today the engine roster includes one more steamer and two diesels, and the railway runs most of the year except in January. Ravenglass terminus is the operational base with offices, sheds and workshops alongside the main-line station; the village was once a Roman naval base at the end of the Roman road through Hardknott Pass and Eskdale.

Below: **WHITEHAVEN** Haig Colliery was the last coal mine in Cumberland, employing 1,800 men in the 1960s. In this picture on 19 June 1969 we see a train of National Coal Board tip wagons being loaded with coal at the coal screening plant, which sorted the coal into different sizes. In the background are two pithead winding frames to work the lifts underground and the colliery main building housing the boilers, engine room, ventilation plant, stores and offices. In the foreground the junk heap of scrap iron and old railway sleepers would be called modern sculpture today. The colliery closed in 1986 as a result of a dangerous geological fault, but the main building and one winding frame survives as the Haig Colliery Mining Museum. The rest of the buildings and the railways have gone.

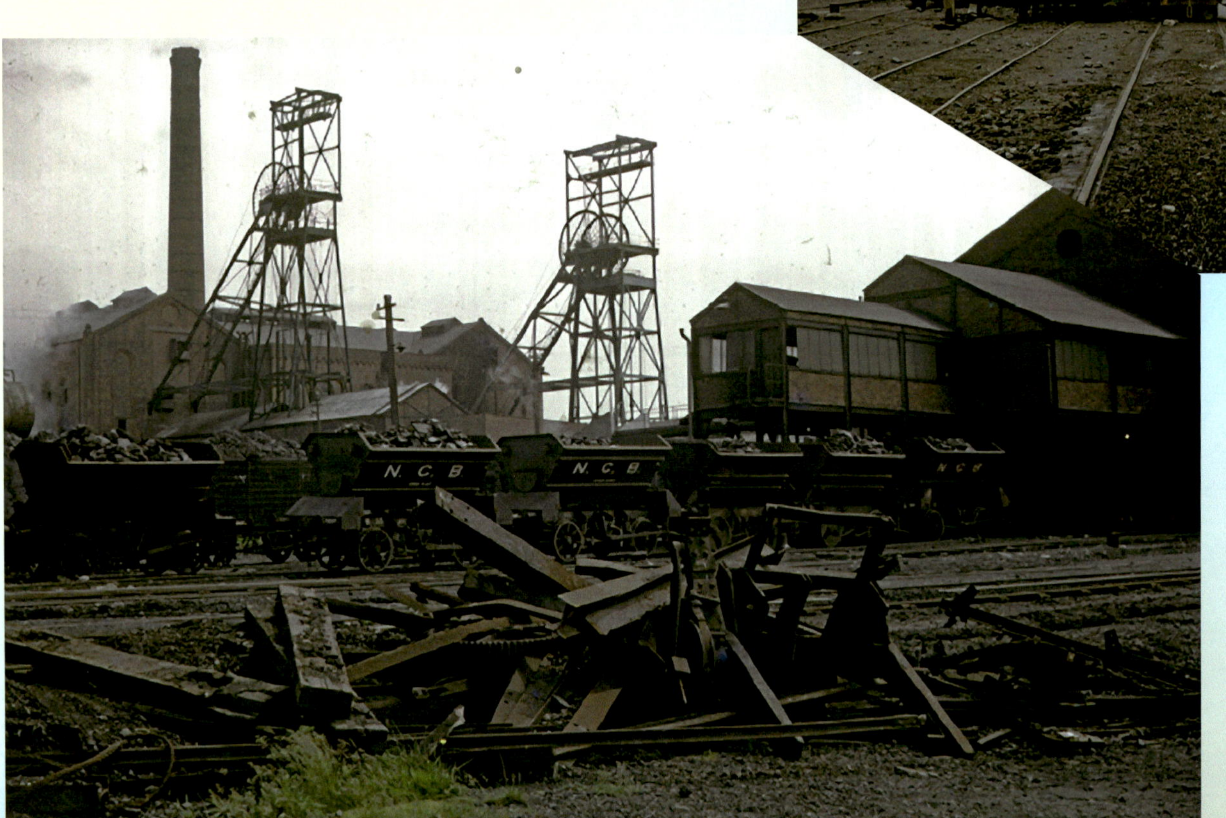

Above: **WHITEHAVEN** Noise, coal dust and steam surround the coal screening plant as railway wagons are loaded with coal sorted by size, and an 0-4-0 saddle tank engine stands by the control room on 5 May 1969.

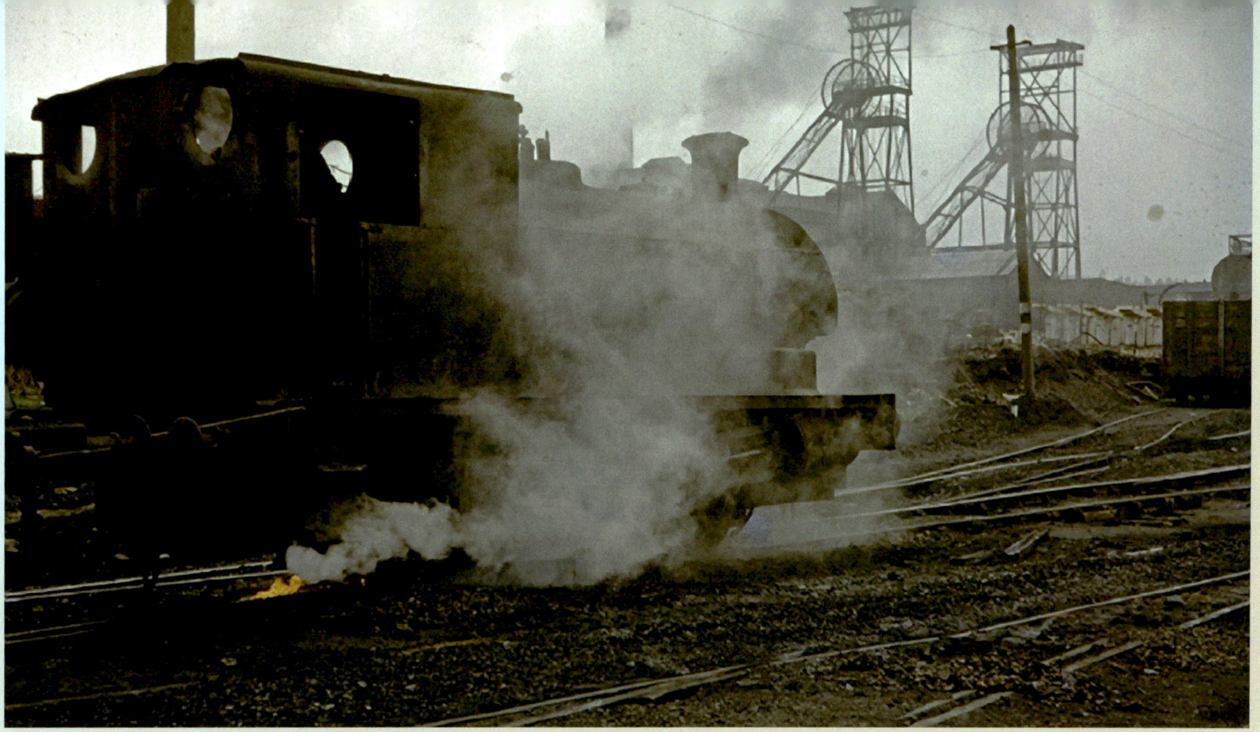

Right: **WHITEHAVEN**
Industrial steam: the fireman of NCB 0-4-0 saddle tank *Solway*, built by Hudswell Clark in 1948, is cleaning out his fire grate at Haig Colliery on 5 May 1969 with two colliery winding frames in the background.

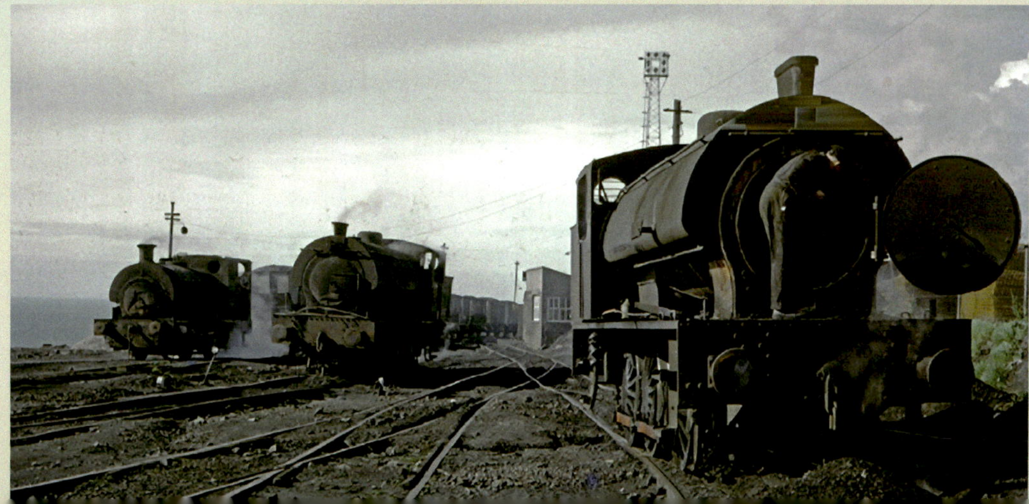

Right: **WHITEHAVEN** A trio of NCB saddle tank engines stand at Haig Colliery on 19 June 1969, including two 0-6-0s with narrow Giesl ejectors designed to reduce coal consumption. In the right foreground the fireman of 0-6-0 locomotive *Revenge* is cleaning his smokebox and burying the track in cinders and soot. On the left the 0-4-0 *Solway* is backing down on to a train of loaded coal wagons. The brick hut was the weighbridge house.

WHITEHAVEN *Solway* on the Solway: the NCB 0-4-0ST runs along the clifftop on the brink of the Solway Firth on 19 June 1969 with a train of empty trucks from the harbour to the washing plant at the former Ladysmith Colliery, 1½ miles south, to be loaded with more washed coal for the harbour. On the left is the west pier and lighthouse, built by John Rennie in 1823-38 to protect the harbour entrance. To the left of the locomotive we see the top of the ventilation shaft of 1840 of the former Wellington Colliery.

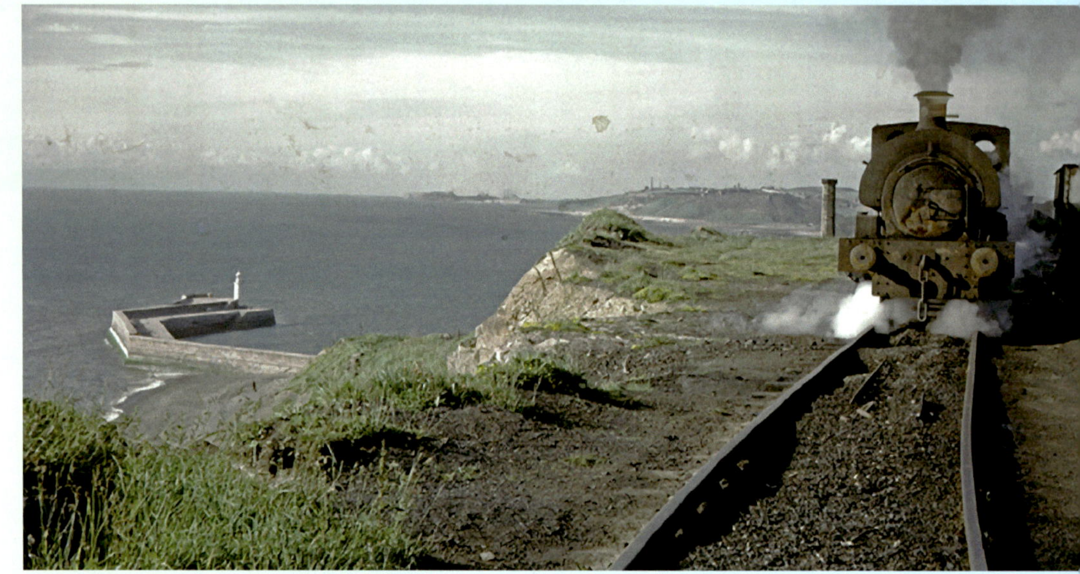

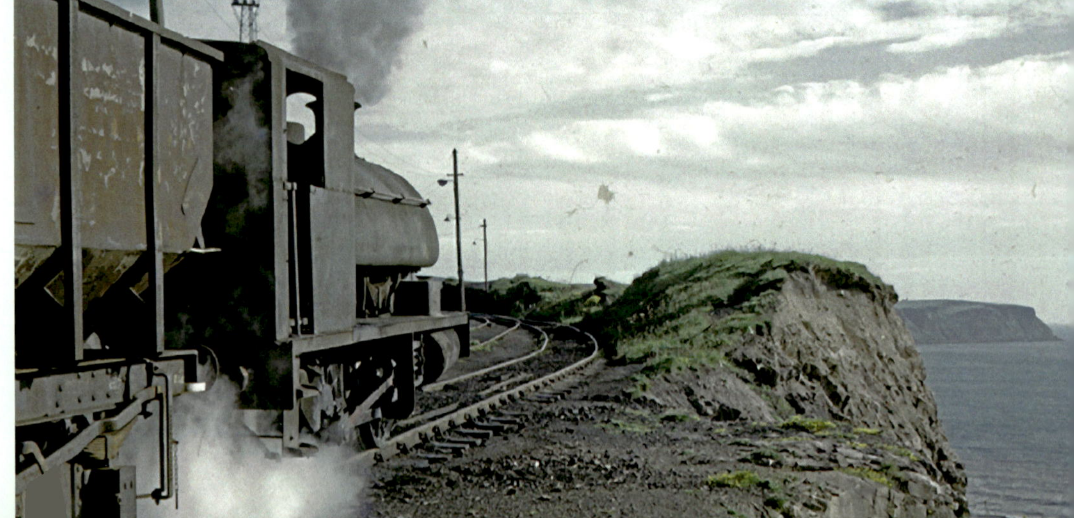

WHITEHAVEN On the same day *Solway* makes its way south along the cliffside from Haig Colliery with empty trucks from the harbour for Ladysmith washing plant, with St Bee's Head in the right background.

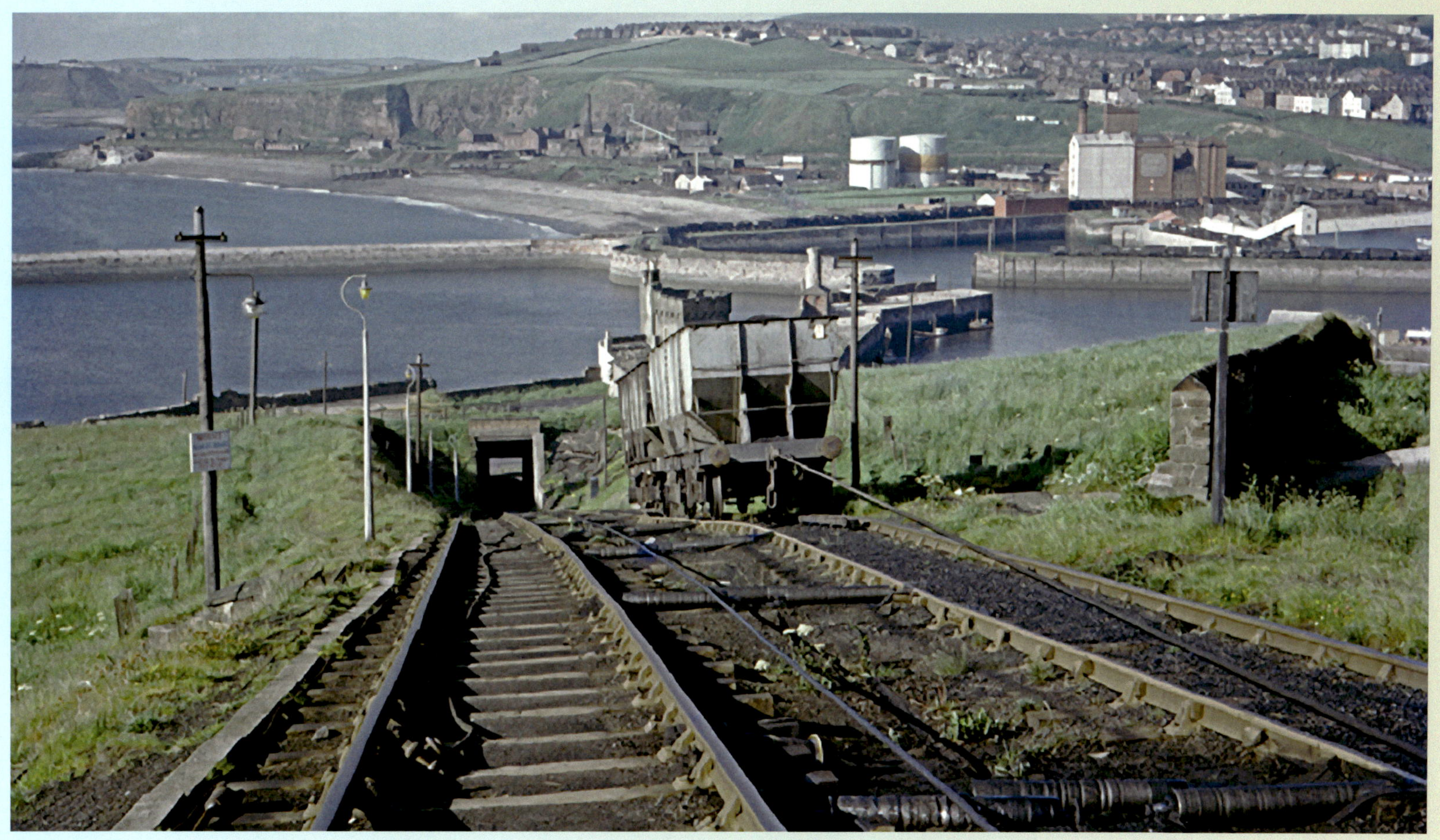

WHITEHAVEN This 1 in 5 cable incline was the link for coal wagons between Haig Colliery and Whitehaven harbour. The cable was worked by an electric winding engine house at the top and the weight of the loaded wagons descending (pictured) was offset by the empties from the harbour hooked on to the other end of the cable. In this view from the top of the incline we see the harbour laid out below with trucks of coal lining the piers awaiting shipment. We also see the Quaker Oats mill on the east pier, the gas works and a disused colliery at the foot of the cliffs north of the harbour. The mill closed in 1972 and in the same year Howgill Brake stopped working because of a landslip and the railway trucks used Corkickle Brake instead till 1975, when the coal went by road.

Right: **CARLISLE** Seven main-line railways converged on the border city of Carlisle in pre-Grouping days and the city is surrounded by a network of freight lines avoiding Citadel main-line passenger station. Here, from St Nicholas Bridge on the southern approaches, we see ex-LMSR 'Black Five' No 44792 (Horwich, 1947) with a northbound freight on 10 April 1964.

Below: **CARLISLE CITADEL** station (left) was named after the Citadel (right), both forming two sides of Court Square and pictured here on 28 May 1961. The twin circular towers flank the English Gate in the south wall of the city; the Scotch Gate was on the north wall. The original Citadel towers of 1541-53 were rebuilt in red sandstone in 1804-11 as the Law Courts, which they were at the time of this photograph; they are now the head office of Cumbria County Council. The statue is that of William, first Earl of Lonsdale, who initiated the

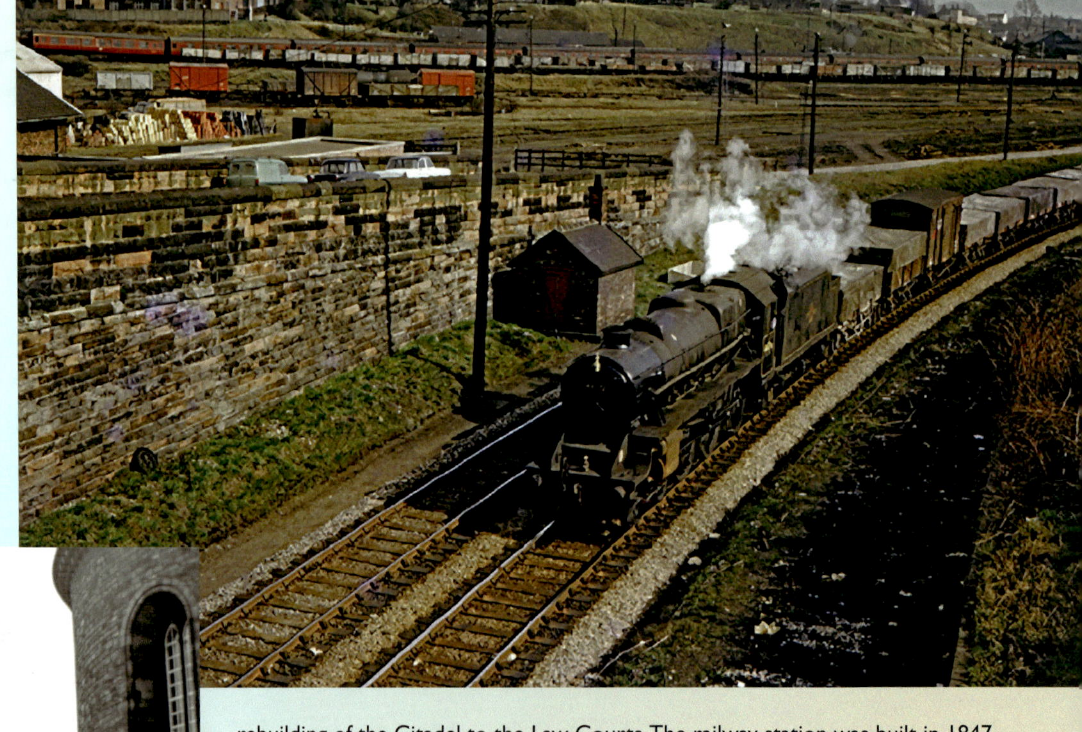

rebuilding of the Citadel to the Law Courts. The railway station was built in 1847 in neo-Tudor grey stonework by Sir William Tite, architect to both the Lancaster & Carlisle Railway and the Caledonian Railway, the original joint owners of the station. The east front is non-symmetrical with a buttressed, lantern clock tower and an arcaded stone portico to the left. We can also see the transverse ridge-and-furrow, glazed overall roof spanning the platforms. Sir William also designed Lancaster and Penrith stations, to match the adjacent castles. Before the Grouping, Carlisle was the junction of the London & North Western Railway, the Caledonian Railway, the Midland Railway, the North Eastern Railway, the North British Railway, the Glasgow & South Western Railway, and the Maryport & Carlisle Railway. At the time of this photograph it was the meeting place of British Railways' Midland, North Eastern and Scottish Regions.

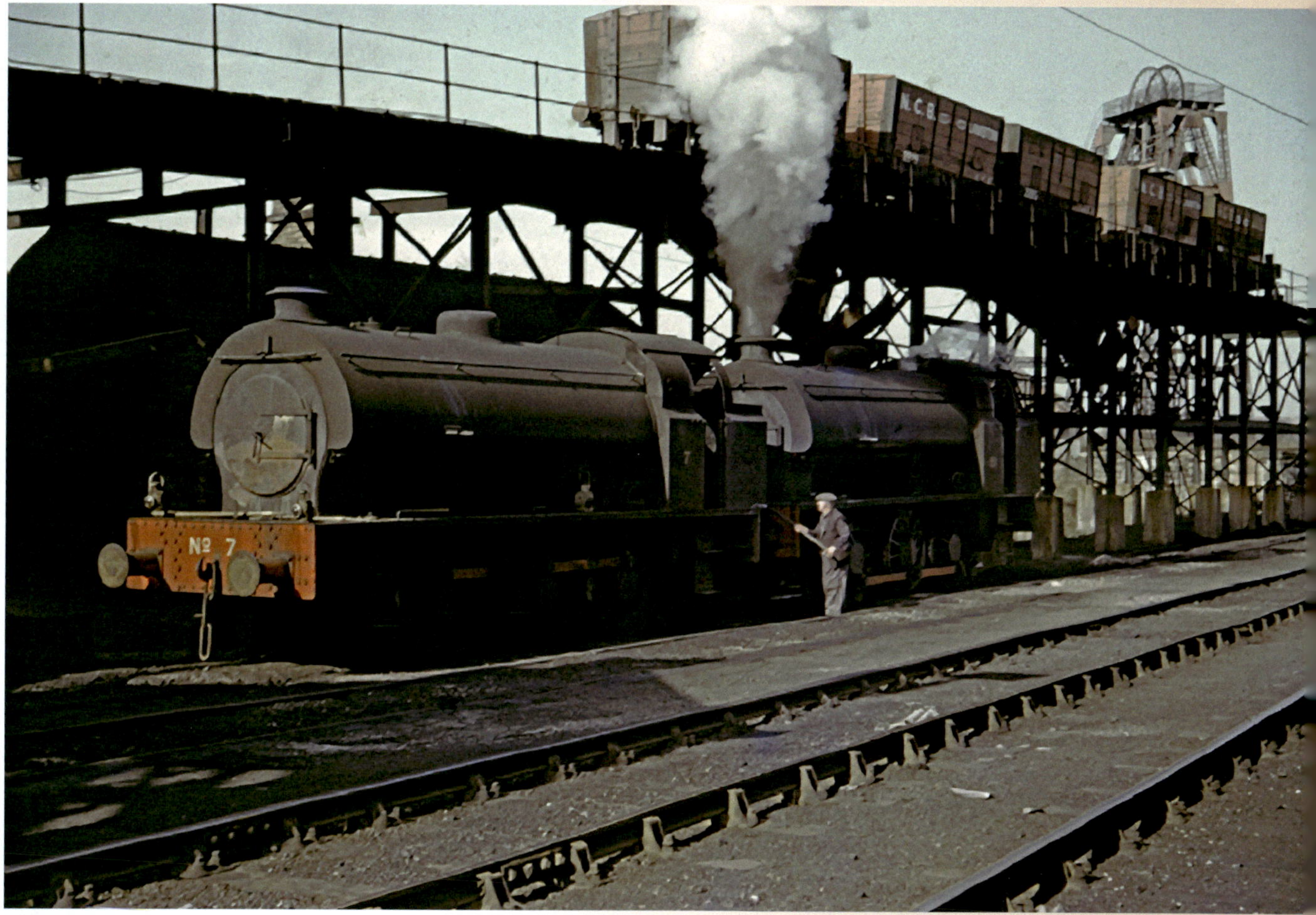

County Durham

PHILADELPHIA, with its loco sheds and workshops, was the hub of the former Lambton Collieries' 70-mile network of railways serving a group of mines between Durham and Sunderland. It was on the line from Herrington Colliery to the BR exchange sidings at Penshaw on the Durham-Sunderland line and the colliery engines had running powers over BR (ex-NER) to deliver the coal to the staithes on the River Wear at Sunderland. The cabs of the locomotives were tapered to fit a small-bore tunnel on the way. In this picture two NCB 0-6-0 saddle tank steam locomotives stand at the coaling stage at Philadelphia on 28 March 1968. The drop-bottom wagons on the ramped pier dropped coal down chutes to the locomotive bunkers in the same way as ships were loaded at the staithes on the river. Behind the ramp is the winding frame for the Dorothea pit.

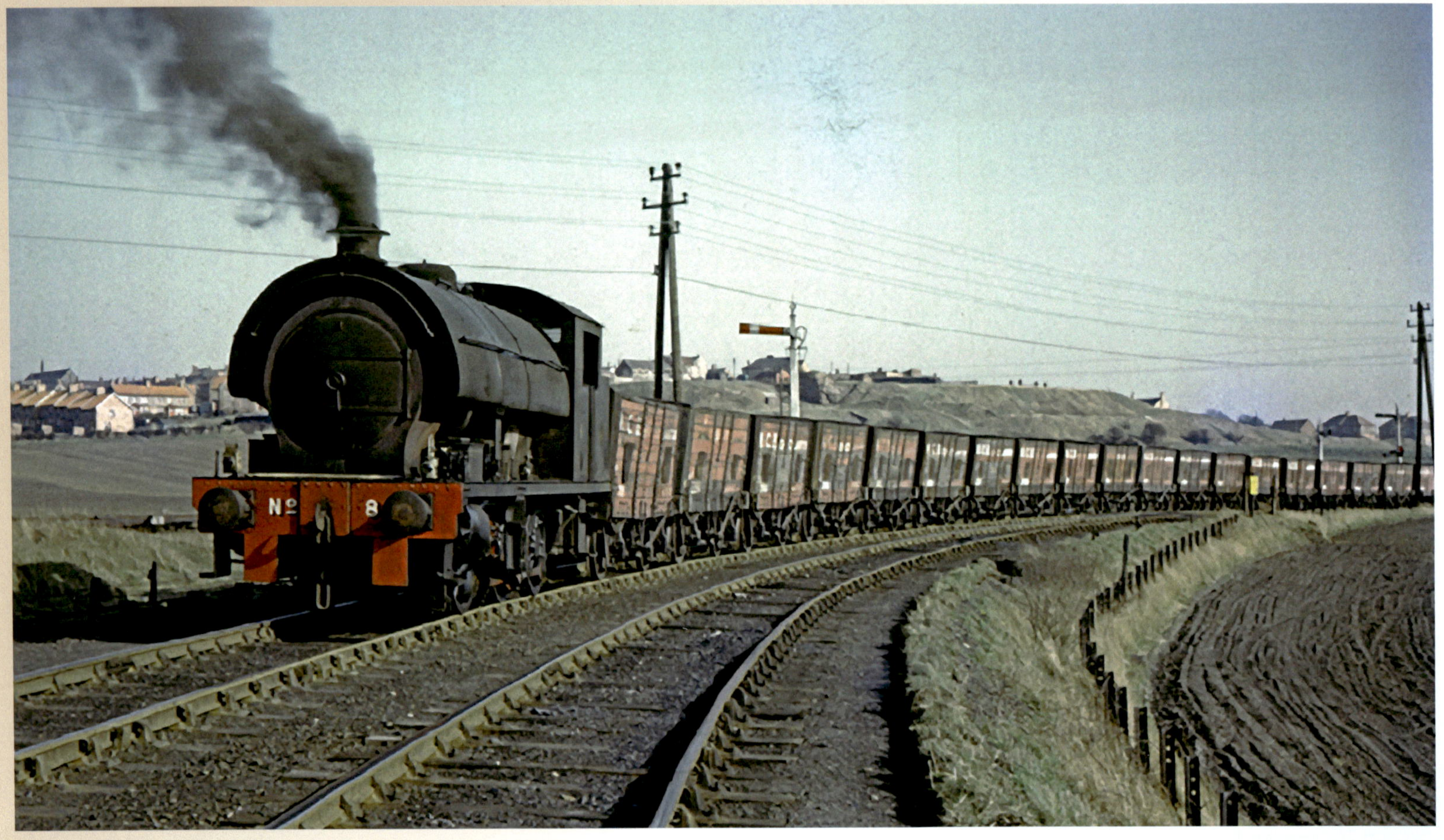

PHILADELPHIA NCB locomotive No 8 propels a train of empty coal wagons around the curve at Philadelphia Bank Top Junction on its way from Penshaw marshalling yard to Houghton Colliery on the same day. The third leg of this triangular junction led to Philadelphia Works and Herrington Colliery. Steam engines pottered around Philadelphia for only one more year before they were replaced by ex-BR 0-6-0 diesel shunters in 1969. The locomotive repair shops closed in 1987 and the general workshops in 1989. County Durham had 127 mines employing 108,000 colliers when the National Coal Board took over in 1947. The last mine to close was at Monkwearmouth in 1994.

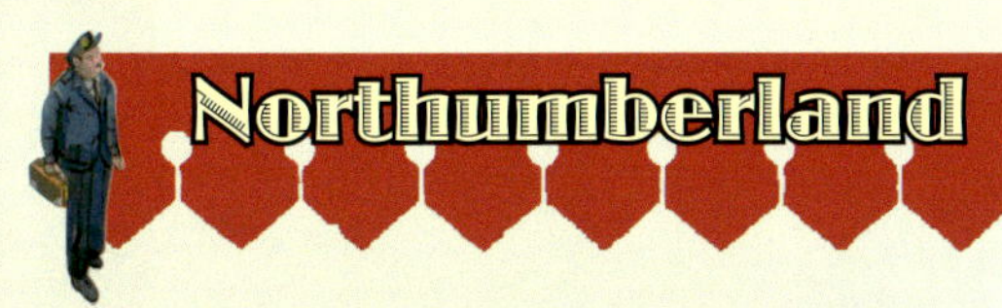

NEWCASTLE is a city of dramatic, high-level bridges. Less photographed than those spanning the river is this stone-arch railway bridge leaping high over The Side at its junction with Dean Street, from which this picture was taken on 28 March 1970. Dean Street was built in the 1780s to succeed the steep and narrow ascent of The Side on the Great North Road route from the old Tyne bridge to the city centre at a time when packhorses were giving way to horse-drawn waggons. The bridge in this picture was built in 1848-49 to carry the York, Newcastle & Berwick Railway, now part of the East Coast Main Line. The prominent building in the background is the Moot Hall, built in 1810-11 for the Northumberland County Courts.

Dean Street was incorporated into the bold and imaginative new city centre built between 1825 and 1840 by architect John Dobson and builder Richard Grainger – a city of broad, main streets and classical buildings laid out to theatrical effect and sensitively superimposed on the medieval town of steep streets and steps. Dean Street leads uphill to Grey Street, terminating in the columnar monument to Earl Grey, the focal point of the city. Dobson's city centre is quite well preserved and Dean Street looks much the same today. The bridge and buildings have been cleaned to reveal the ochre colour of the stonework. The Moot Hall is now used only for public functions and weddings and as a period film set.

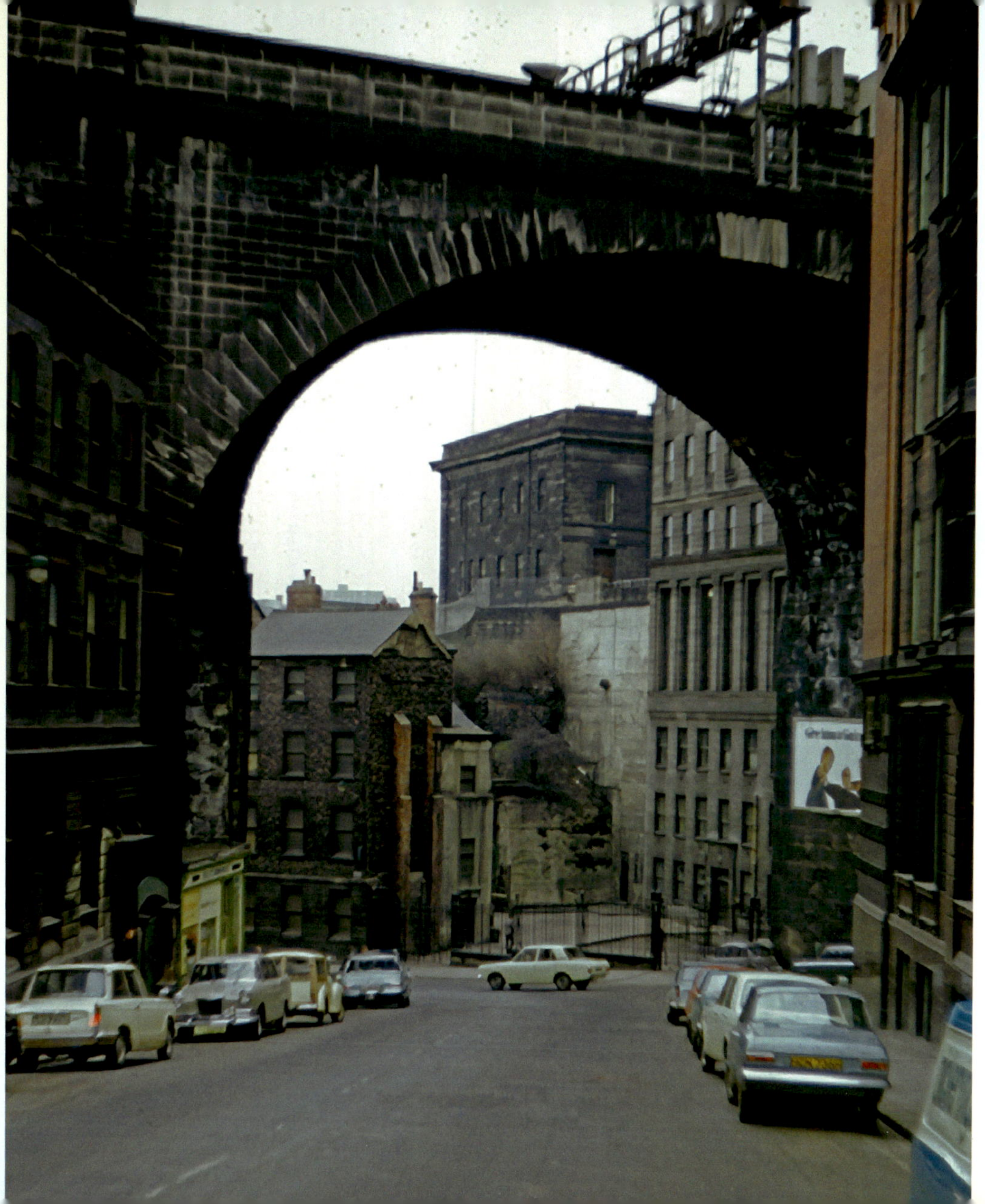

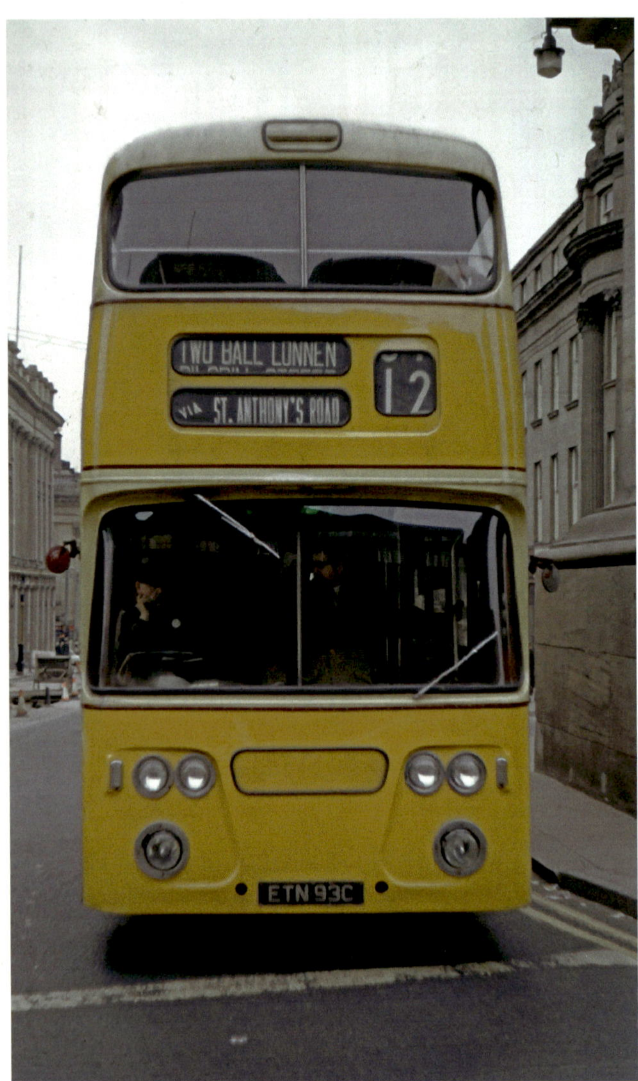

Left: **NEWCASTLE** At the top of Grey Street, by now with clean buildings, one of the Tyneside PTE's Alexander-bodied Leyland Atlantean buses of 1965 pauses at the signals beside the Earl Grey monument on 28 March 1970. The word 'lonnen' on the destination blind is from a dialect word for a 'lane', which is at Fenham; the word is 'loan' in Scotland. Newcastle buses were blue and white from 1912 until 1949, when they began to be repainted in yellow and cream. The trolleybuses were yellow with brown/maroon bands from 1935, so when nine Bournemouth trolleybuses were loaned to Newcastle from 1942 to 1945 they merged unobtrusively into the fleet. The brown bands disappeared from 1949 and the yellow paintwork went through an orangey phase before reverting to yellow as seen here.

Right: **BERWICK** The border at Berwick was also the border between the territories of English and Scottish bus companies, but they shared the same premises. Here is the joint bus station and garage of United Automobile Services of Darlington and the Scottish Motor Traction Company of Edinburgh, photographed on 29 May 1959 with buses of those two companies respectively left and right. On the left is a 1949 Eastern-bodied Bristol L loading for Ord, Horncliffe and Norham in Northumberland, and on the right is a 1956 Alexander-bodied AEC Reliance destined for St Abbs via Eyemouth on the Berwickshire coast. Berwick was the last outpost of the Bristol L type on United in 1966. The bus station has since been replaced by a new library and three shops fronting Marygate, and Berwick has no bus station today.

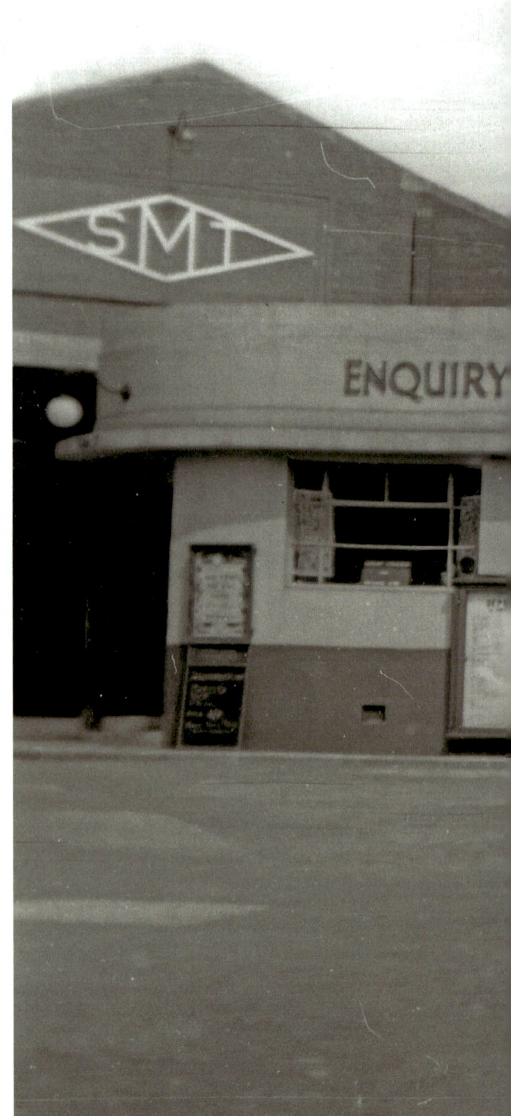

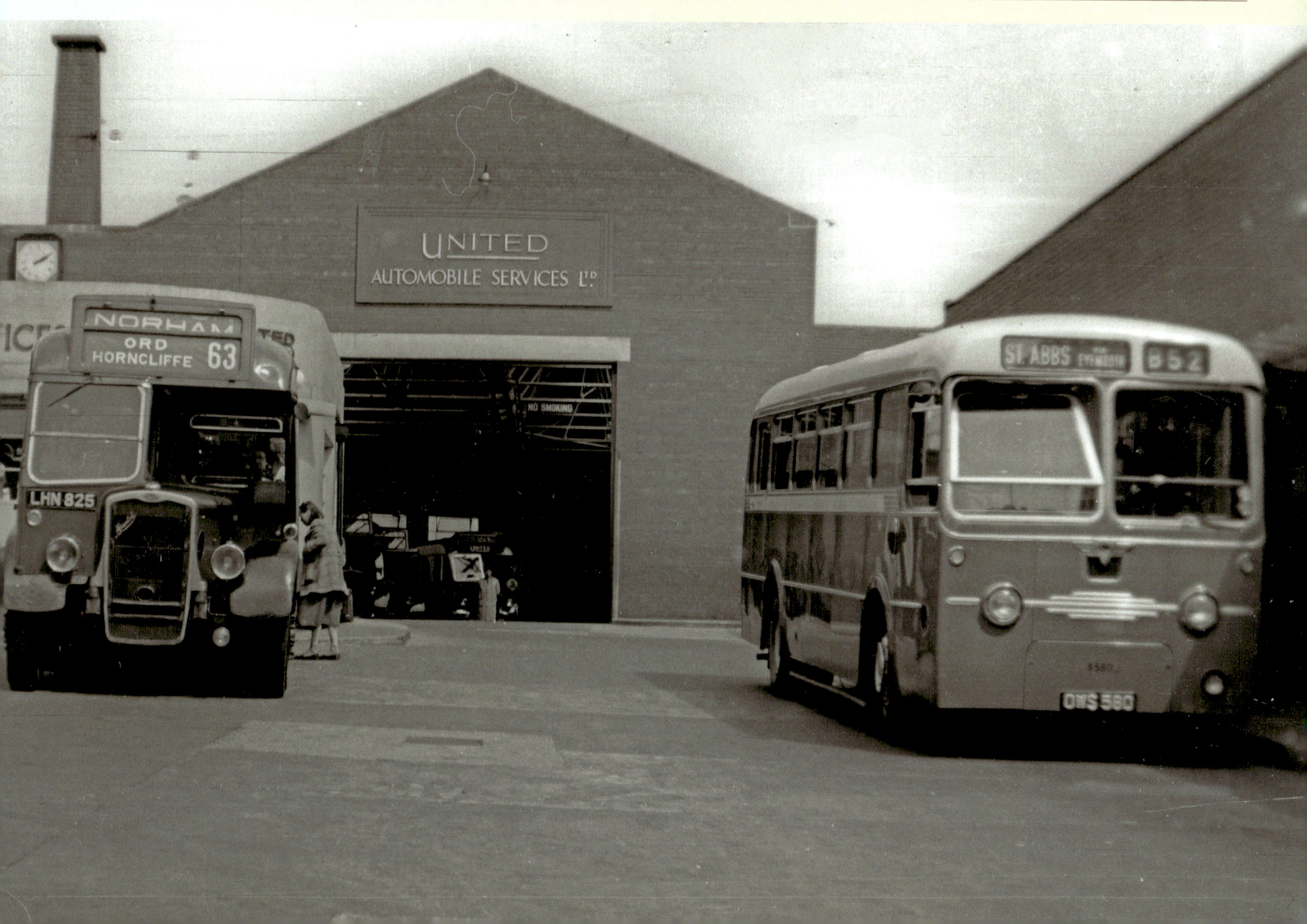
UNITED
AUTOMOBILE SERVICES L^TD
NORHAM
ORD
HORNCLIFFE 63
LHN 825
NO SMOKING
ST. ABBS 52
OWS 580

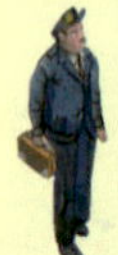

Index of locations

Ais Gill 38
Beauchief 20
Berwick 62-63
Bradford 30-31
Brightside 24
Carlisle 58
Dalegarth 53
Dallam 40
Dent 36-37

Dent Head 34
Dentdale 35
Garsdale 37
Grayrigg 42
Haig Colliery 12-13, 54-57
Halton 28
Hull 4, 14-15
Kendal 9-12, 46-47
Leeds 6-8, 25-27
Lonsdale 1, 41
Mallerstang 39

Meadowhead 17
Millom 51-52
Muncaster 53
Newcastle 13, 61-62
Norton Woodseats 3, 18-19
Oxenholme 43-45
Philadelphia 59-60
Ravenglass & Eskdale Railway 12, 53
Ribblehead 33-34
Rotherham 4, 16
Settle-Carlisle railway 8-9, 33-39

Sheffield 4-6, 21-23
Staveley 48
Teesside 32
Temple Newsam 29
Ullswater 50
Whitehaven 12-13, 54-57
Windermere 49

The Transport Travelogue series *(Volume numbers shown refer to the Recollections series numbering)*

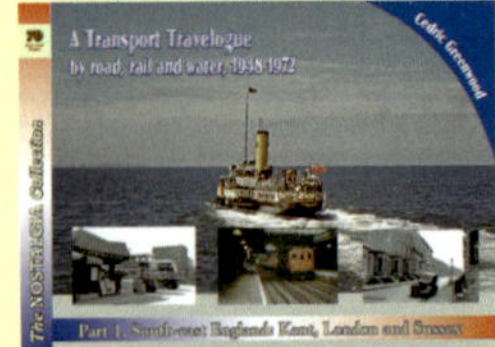

Vol 70: A Transport Travelogue by road rail and water, 1948-1972
Part 1, South-east England: Kent, London and Sussex

July 2018		*By Cedric Greenwood*
169 x 238mm	64pp	c60col/b&w
ISBN: 978 1 85794 503 4	Softcover	£8.00

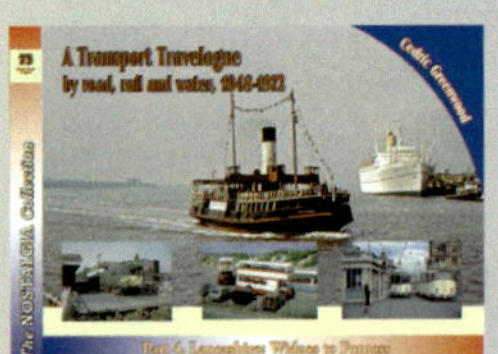

Vol 73: A Transport Travelogue by road rail and water, 1948-1972
Part 4, Lancashire: Widnes to Furness

July 2018		*By Cedric Greenwood*
169 x 238mm	64pp	c60col/b&w
ISBN: 978 1 85794 499 0	Softcover	£8.00

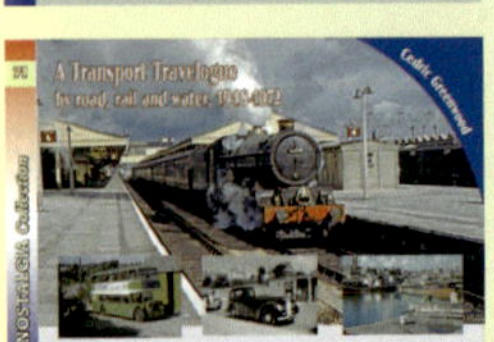

Vol 71: A Transport Travelogue by road rail and water, 1948-1972
Part 2, South and South West England: Wessex to Cornwall

July 2018		*By Cedric Greenwood*
169 x 238mm	48pp	c60col/b&w
ISBN: 978 1 85794 502 7	Softcover	£6.00

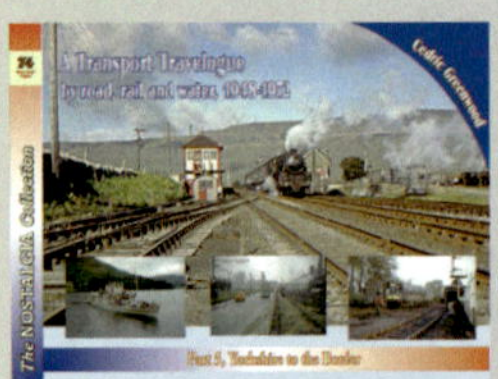

Vol 74: A Transport Travelogue by road rail and water, 1948-1972
Part 5, Yorkshire to the Border

July 2018		*By Cedric Greenwood*
169 x 238mm	64pp	c60col/b&w
ISBN: 978 1 85794 501 0	Softcover	£8.00

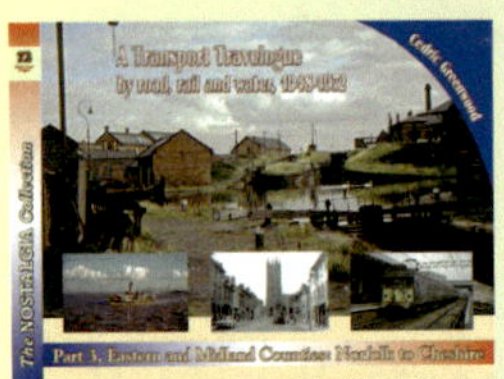

Vol 72: A Transport Travelogue by road rail and water, 1948-1972
Part 3, Eastern and Midland Counties: Norfolk to Cheshire

July 2018		*By Cedric Greenwood*
169 x 238mm	64pp	c60col/b&w
ISBN: 978 1 85794 504 1	Softcover	£8.00

Vol 94: A Transport Travelogue by road rail and water, 1948-1972
Part 6: Wales, Man and Scotland

July 2018		*By Cedric Greenwood*
169 x 238mm	64pp	c60col/b&w
ISBN: 978 1 85794 500 3	Softcover	£8.00